Bounce-Up™

Bounce-Up:

Outpower Adversity, Boost Resilience, Rebound Higher

By Mj Callaway, CSP

Library of Congress Cataloging-in-Publication Data:

Callaway, Mj

> Bounce-Up™: Outpower Adversity, Boost Resilience, Rebound Higher/Mj Callaway

> Includes bibliographical references

> Includes index

> ISBN: 978-1-7342649-9-9

Printed in the United States of America

Dedication

To my family and Power Teams:

I have Bounced-Up™ higher and stronger because of you!

To everyone who has faced or is facing a setback,

may you build your own Power Team.

Table of Contents

Foreword
Dr. Renee Thompson

As a nurse for almost 30 years, I've seen my share of devastation. From 18-year-olds who go to the emergency department with a headache only to learn they have a brain tumor and won't live more than a year to the 54-year-old with a wife and two kids who suffers an abrupt, hemorrhagic stroke and won't ever talk, walk, or feed himself again.

I've seen more suffering than most. But like the phoenix that emerges out of the fiery ashes, I've also seen firsthand the power of the human spirit to rise above.

Most humans experience loss, setbacks, or significant life-altering events at some point in their lives. For some people, these experiences are devastating as they completely and irrevocably alter someone's life plan. Someone abruptly loses a child or spouse; goes in for a routine physical exam and is told they have cancer; gets fired from a job without warning; or learns their spouse is having an affair. We've all experienced potentially life-altering events or at least know someone who has.

When experiencing a devastating, life-altering event, there emerge two different kinds of people. The first kind become paralyzed by the event and succumb to the heavy burden of the loss or change. They seem to forever define the rest of their lives by that one event. The event becomes their new identity.

And then there are people like Mj.

I met Mj several years ago during a National Speaker's Association local chapter meeting in Pittsburgh. I can remember two things about Mj: she was smiling and she was wearing purple. Very quickly, I knew that Mj was someone I wanted in my circle of positive influencers, and before long, Mj joined a mastermind group Kathy Parry and I started a few years before.

As I was getting to know Mj, it seemed as though she lived a "perfect" life. She was growing a successful speaking business, had a beautiful family, shared time with a great group of friends (as evidenced by her Facebook page), and was always smiling.

And then one day during our mastermind meeting, she casually dropped, "My ex-husband tried to run me over with his truck." She said it so matter-of-fact that I laughed — thought she was kidding. But Mj was telling the truth. She then shared how she left with only $500 to her name, had to live with friends for a while, and took a sales job but didn't make any sales for quite some time. Wow!

She then talked about how she didn't let him or that situation define her and how she "bounced-up."

But it was when she casually mentioned she was diagnosed with cancer that Mj transformed and earned the credibility to write this book. I've never seen someone month after month maintain such positivity despite receiving a potentially devastating diagnosis as Mj.

At the exact same time, I had another friend with the exact same diagnosis, yet the way she handled it was the complete opposite as Mj.

Mj chose to take control over her situation (at least what she could control).

My friend allowed the cancer to control her. Mj even offered to talk with my friend, but she declined.

Mj learned everything she could about equipping her body to fight the cancer by eating extremely healthy, getting the rest she needed, and maintaining an exercise program.

My friend ate junk food and vegetated on the couch.

Mj chose to be positive despite losing her hair, gaining weight, losing weight, gaining, losing. She even modeled her newest wig at one of our meetings—of course, sporting a fancy purple jacket too.

My friend stayed in the house because she had no hair.

I can't think of anyone more qualified to write this book than Mj, who lives and breathes how to bounce-up from setbacks.

Bouncing up is about choosing the type of life you want despite the events that occur along the way. It's about saying "hello" to the fear and "verbal drama" yet moving forward anyway. Like a rubber ball, when you hit the floor, the kinds of people who are able to push through and thrive are the ones, like Mj, who find a way to **BOUNCE UP!**

Dr. Renee Thompson
CEO & Founder of the Healthy Workforce Institute

Message from Mj: Behind the Smile

"Rainbows come after the rain. See the good about to surface." – **Mjism**

Setbacks happen for a reason. It's the speedbump in our journey of life. When hardships occur, we have a choice and a path to travel. We become stronger after a setback.

I know what it's like to be immobilized by circumstances and unsure which direction is the right direction to take. I've wrestled the inner head talk that can flip on as suddenly and dangerous as a lightning bolt.

I understand fear. Fear that grips you when you get a dire diagnosis, and you wonder how you will work as a single person and solopreneur.

I might not have experienced what you're going through right now, or what you've endured. I have experienced adversity, heartache, loss, and starting over—more than once.

I rebuilt my personal and professional life without a significant settlement. I had $500 and some personal belongings. What I had was a support group, which became my Power Team. While dealing with this adversity, I became one of the top five sales executives, selling three times my sales quota.

I've survived an illness that threatened my life. One that zapped my energy, making even the simplest actions like getting off the sofa drain every bit of your strength, and distorts your physical appearance. However, this setback unintentionally made me pivot and gave me a new brand and a new niche.

I've reinvented my professional life three times in less than one decade.

I wrote this book to help others get up after they've hit the ground, increase their resilience, gain momentum, and create a new positive "normal" so that they can Bounce-Up™ higher and stronger.

Even though you can't always control what life throws your way, you can control how you Bounce-Up™ from the curveballs life throws unexpectedly.

Here's to your rainbow after the rain, good things after the bad stuff, and Bouncing-Up higher and stronger!

Let's Outpower Adversity, Boost Resilience and Bounce-Up™ together!

Mj Callaway

How to Use This Book

Throughout Bounce-Up, you'll find sections that will help you outpower adversity and build momentum so that you can bounce-up.

 Power Buzz shares additional resources.

 Behind-the-Scenes reveal actions taken to Bounce-Up.

 Success Bound provides activities for you to do that are "all about you."

 Game Changers offer techniques, tactics, and tips to crush change.

 Bounce-Up Momentum recaps Chapter actions you can take to build momentum.

 Bounce-Up Power shows you how others outpowered adversity.

 Boost Your Bounce-Up Factor provides key questions to ignite ideas and actions so that you can rebound higher!

Part I

Devious Roadblocks

CHAPTER 1
You've Taken a Face-Plant in the Middle of Your Life

"A setback becomes the directional signal to pivot." **- Mjism**

Life has a way of hurling setbacks straight at you during the most inopportune time. Not that there is ever a good time for adversity. Life's difficulties seem to know when you're down, and the challenges keep coming like massive waves crashing on the beach during a tropical storm.

Hard times cause disruptions, disappointments, and heartache. One unexpected event can disrupt your career, family, or life. Adversity disrupts your life because what you once knew has been taken away. Setbacks create roadblocks because you lose something during or after the difficulties.

Power Buzz:
Face-Plants Hit Americans

You might be one of the fortunate ones who hasn't hit a hardship yet. What's crazy is 92 percent of Americans report they have suffered at least one significant negative event in their lives, according to the National Opinion Research Center at University of Chicago.

You can't get around it. Everyone will face difficulties in life. The intensity of that challenge is relative to each individual. Some people face a traffic jam with anger, while others will suffer the most challenging time of their lives with grace and a smile.

Maybe you're reading this book because you're stuck in the same place, and you realize you don't want to be in this place. You want to move forward. Recognizing the roadblocks that cause you to stay in the same place week after week, month after month, year after year is the first step to *Bounce-Up*™.

Whether you're stuck from a past disappointment or facing adversity, the issue is setbacks steal something essential from us. Your setback could be personal or professional. Either way, your personal disruption impacts your professional life and vice versa. Unfortunately, loss turns out to be a common thread.

Setbacks Steal

Setbacks can impact you emotionally, financially, mentally, physically, spiritually, and socially. Maybe you've faced one of these common setbacks:

- Loss of business or a sale you thought you would get
- Job loss or missed promotion
- Rejection, whether it's business rejection or a personal rejection
- Loss of a co-worker, boss, or client who was your champion or role model
- Decrease in business
- Business merger that disrupts your company's infrastructure
- Company relocates to another space or state
- DUI or a suspension or loss of license
- Addiction, losing control in one or more areas
- Loss of health due to illness or an accident
- Loss of a loved one through a breakup, divorce, or death

Although the setback list can go on, the nitty-gritty comes down to this—adversity deals a loss. You lose one of the following:

- Loss of Innocence
- Loss of Identity
- Loss of Control
- Loss of Support
- Loss of Confidence
- Loss of Familiarity (also known as Comfort or What's Comfortable)
- Loss of Love
- Loss of Security
- Loss of Resources (financial, housing)
- Loss of Health

Adversity Shapes You

Adversity can be multi-pronged, meaning it affects multiple areas of your life. For example, being downsized from your job will alter your lifestyle, bank account, emotional well-being, and/or physical self.

When we view adversity as a signal, it changes our perspective. Setbacks give you the reason to alter your career path, habits, routines, and life plans.

Twice in the past nine years, I've faced life-threatening events, which I'll share in our journey together. I had to start over with next to nothing in the way of financial resources to discover how rich I was with the support of family and friends. I've had doors close on career positions that led to a different path I certainly would not have chosen if adversity never happened. My current business transpired as a result of on-site project errors caused mostly by Mother Nature in my former career.

Though we want to avoid difficulties at all costs, when we do this, we stay stuck in passivity. We're comfortable where we are. Without adversity, we remain in the same place. Sometimes we allow roadblocks to shackle us from moving forward. Those three roadblocks are <u>Fear</u>, <u>Verbal Drama</u>, and <u>Immobility</u>, which I coined the Sticky Monster Ball, Superball, and Hacky Sack Syndrome.

Challenges allow us a chance to grow, pivot, or shift. Growing takes us to new opportunities we would never get to experience without that challenge.

Some losses can convert into an opportunity and others into a legacy with new traditions. How is it possible to turn it into an "opportunity"? By viewing your loss as an "opportunity" rather than a "loss," you're able to see it from a different perspective. You'll meet several people in Part III who did exactly that—they turned a loss into an opportunity.

The dilemma, or problem, isn't the hardship dealt to you. The dilemma becomes your perspective of the adversity. Adversity shapes you. Adversity makes you stronger.

Remember, Kelly Clarkson's song *Stronger*? This one line nails it, *"What doesn't kill you makes you stronger."*

Game Changer:
Get Back Up

Face-plants do not need to define you. Use these tips to take the first steps to shift.

1. Give yourself kudos for taking the first step by reading *Bounce-Up*. Reading this book shows you're ready to discover the opportunity within the chaos. Get going!
2. Connect with someone who has already experienced the same setback as you. However, this person needs to be

one who overcame it. Meaning, he or she has taken the hit and successfully moved on. Get the inside scoop by asking what positive outcome happened because of the face-plant.

3. Listen to Rocky Balboa's talk with his son. Do a simple Google search for Rocky's speech to his son. Afterward, ask yourself, have you moved forward with the hit?

Bounce-Up Momentum

- Recognize your setback.
- Pinpoint the loss experienced.
- Understand how it affected you emotionally, financially, mentally, physically, spiritually, or socially.
- Reflect on who else was involved.
- Think about one positive outcome that has occurred because of the setback.
- Consider what opportunity this adversity can create.
- Take one action at a time to build momentum.

Boost Your Bounce-Up Factor: Face Your Setbacks

Define the most significant setback and the loss it caused.

1. What setback happened?
2. How did the setback affect you?
3. What loss occurred?
4. What is one takeaway you gained from this chapter?
5. What is one positive action you will take?

Bounce-Up Wordology

Bounce-Up Factor: Your ability to overcome setbacks, handle risk, improvise options, pause during disruptions, and remain positive.

Sticky Monster Ball, Superball, and Hacky Sack Syndrome: A fun analogy using three kid toys to compare the three roadblocks—Fear, Verbal Drama, and Immobility—that keep you from bouncing up after a setback.

Author's Note: Mental health is a broad topic, which this book does not cover. These tips are not meant to replace a person's need for medical care. For anxiety or other serious health issues, please consult your physician immediately. Please consult the back of the book for additional professional resources.

CHAPTER 2
Lose the Grip with Fear

"Snuggled in your comfort zone can be a bigger risk than taking your first step." – **Mjism**

What makes the difference between Bouncing-Up and defeat? Whatever you're doing right now, it isn't about the position, the job description, or the title. When I sold custom homes for a national site builder, it wasn't the home (or in this situation the blueprint) I was selling, it was the vision of an individual, a couple, or a family's dream; their idea of what they thought would make a happy home, one that they would share with extended family and friends. The house they wanted to walk down the sidewalk, insert their key in the door with a smile and think, "I'm so glad to be home." The place they would watch their family grow and share a lifetime of love and joy.

In working with my clients, the ultimate goal became giving them the place where they could create a lifetime of happy memories. In the end, the perspective determined my success. It was never about building the house. It was making the blueprint work for the family's lifestyle.

Behind-the-Scene with Mj:
Look for Opportunity

When I first started with the company, I was in the midst of my first life-altering event when an alcohol addiction got the better of my former spouse and he tried to drive into me with his truck. Okay, I'm putting it mildly. I left a 20-plus year marriage with $500 and some personal belongings. I spent a month living with a girlfriend until I could pull together a plan. I didn't know anything about building a custom home. I had taken the position with an on-your-site builder because I knew I could sell, and with the commission-based pay scale, I could make more money. The more I sold, the more I would make. The opportunity to make more money was very appealing as I still had one child in college, and I needed to rebuild my life.

Take a Risk

For all those reasons, it made sense when I accepted the position, but it didn't afterward because I couldn't read blueprints. I didn't know anything about foundations, house wrap, or land preparation. During the interview when the sales director asked if I knew what a header and footer were, I said, "Yes," because I thought he was talking about a word document. Yes, that's how oblivious I was to reading blueprints.

I didn't know anything about square footage, gravel tonnage, or perk tests. My location didn't have a model home to show customers. I worked out of a storefront. Yes, a storefront. Think a small retail space in a strip plaza. Think about this, who accepts a commission-based position when your bank account shows low funds? It's like driving on an expressway with an empty tank.

Determined, I memorized the mandatory script and put that dialogue into practice. At this point, I'd love to share that the script had a secret code and buyers stood in line to sign contracts. Ha! That script never worked for me. I didn't sell anything when I used that script. Nothing. Zero. Nada.

When you're on a 90-day probation period, with the requirement to sign one contract and a single mom with an almost-empty bank account and a son in his senior year of college, fear creeps in like those pesky ants after the chocolate cake at a summer picnic. Fear causes tense shoulders, clenched muscles, and mounds of stress. Fear zaps your energy. Worst yet, fear is rooted in what does not exist in the present. Think about it. Most often, fears center around an event that hasn't happened.

I shifted my focus. When I started to ask the real heartfelt questions about the family, my conversations changed. My focus changed. My clients changed. My numbers changed.

Questions Can Conquer Fear

Owning "my" questions improved the results. The questions became ones I'd want to be asked as a person and not a number. When I looked at clients as friends, the fear slipped away. Fear drifted away because the focus wasn't on me anymore; it was on the clients.

Fear could've kept me generating the same company sales pitch over and over, falling into an unsuccessful rut. I'll admit it did—at least in the beginning when I followed the script. I asked the company-required questions. The questions that seemed more like a survey than a conversation about a family's home or lifestyle. For almost three months, I recited those scripted questions because of the fear of losing my job, fear of not making the right statements, and fear of having the company's secret shopper catch me. Fear overshadowed my belief in myself and my ability to succeed.

Fear can be useful, too. Fear of losing my job pushed me to make a change. I knew I could **not** continue with the current path. To pivot, I went back to what I knew I did well and that was connecting with people. Focusing on my potential clients, talking about their happy lives, finding out more about them was twofold. One, conversations about my buyers limited my thoughts about my own unsettled life. I couldn't think about them and me at the same time. Two, when I switched the focus, questions, and emotions, I rocked the results! When I left the company, I was the only female sales executive in the top five, selling three times my sales quota. I Bounced-Up. One shift led to another. Now, I didn't do it alone. I pulled in my support team, aka, my Power Team, which you'll read about in Chapter 4.

If I could do it, **you can**, too. Now, let's kick fear out!

Fear Grips Us

Fear grips like one of those sticky balls kids throw against the wall, and it sticks. The kind of toy a child might get in a vending machine. Sometimes, it's a monster face sticky ball, which fits because fear can play games with your mindset the way the monster under the bed sneaks into a child's imagination. The sticky ball grips the wall the way fear grips you. Fear can cause you to make the wrong decision or be indecisive, which becomes a decision after all because we've decided to stay in the same place. Fear blocks the path to what you need to do to Bounce-Up so that you can hit the goals or dreams that will enrich your life.

You know fear appears in challenging times. Fear creeps into a place that can be fun, too. Well, fun for those who love to be scared. Consider haunted houses that open during the Halloween season. You don't know when, yet you know someone at some point will jump out, holding a fake chainsaw or some other weapon. Your heart beats faster than a NASCAR engine. You're slowly moving from room to room. Then, when you least expect it, the unknown happens. Life's uncertainties occur the same way—out of nowhere, fear erupts.

Now, I'm not saying fear will be easy to shrug off. Let's consider one area where fear shows up, getting downsized in the workplace. Being out of work creates a laundry list of concerns and fears. How will you pay your bills? How will you feed your kids? How long will it take to get another job? Will you make the same amount of money? That fear is real. I've been there. Maybe you have, too, or someone you know.

Why Fear Happens

These situations bring in fear instead of opportunity. Opportunity brings in change.

1. A repeat of the past: Repeating a past scenario can stop us from trying again because the thought of having the same results slam into us like a sumo wrestler.
2. The unknown: Uncertainty creates fear. Without knowing the outcome, your mind runs to negative possibilities, and these negative possibilities create fear.
3. Failure: The possibility of failing causes fear. Then, there are all the side effects of failing, from the backlash of what family and friends will say to embarrassment and humiliation. No one wants to fail. Although if we think of it as a lesson learned or an experiment, it can take away some of the risks. As the saying goes, *You never know what you can do unless you try.*

Fear influences the decision-making process and shapes so much of your life.

Fear Strikes in Real-Life Situations

As you read the following real-life events, which caused fear, consider if one of these examples resonates with you.

Real-Life Sales Example: Repeat of the Past

Salespeople often hear *you're only as good as your last sale, week, or month.* Sadly, some leaders promote this attitude. There's always a way to get your groove back. It might take longer than you'd like, however, that day is coming.

While on vacation, a young, top-producing logistics sales representative needed to find a load price while in Disney World with his wife and two small children. He told his customer he would need 20 minutes because he had to get out of line and find a quiet spot. The client went elsewhere. The fear that emerged for this young professional was that he couldn't take a family vacation because he would lose customers.

Real-Life Business Example: The Unknown

As one of the co-owners of a start-up company, Ronald Wayne feared the company's increasing debt, and the possibility of the company failing would cause him to lose his house along with other assets. Fear drove Ronald Wayne to sell his 10 percent share to his two partners. He made $800 from his sale. Today, 10 percent of that company would be worth more than $80 billion. More than likely, you or someone you know bought a product from this "fruity" single-word start-up known to young and young-at-heart as Apple. Crazy when you think about it as you can spend $800 for one Apple product today. Ronald Wayne missed out due to fear.

Real-Life Risk Example: Fear of Failure

During coffee and conversation with a colleague I hadn't see in 20 years, my friend asked, *"Weren't you afraid to start your own business and go out on your own, especially as a single woman? I wouldn't have been able to do it."* Although she had a successful career in academia, fear of the unknown would prevent her from taking a risk.

Sure, I was frightened. By the way, let's consider afraid or frightened as the cousin to fear. (If it is a risk, our brains want us to avoid danger.) However, it was a risk I had taken before when my back was against the wall, so I knew I had made it work once, and I could make it work again. Fear could've stopped me from trying. It didn't because I had faced the same doubt before and won.

Fear Overrides Common Sense

With fear, you can make the wrong decision because you're operating from a fear-based mentality. In simplest terms, our brain senses danger and sends signals to react because our brain is wired to protect us from harm.

- You didn't ask for the raise, promotion, or sale for fear of rejection.
- You stay silent during a committee meeting because you're afraid your boss and colleagues will laugh at your suggestion, or fear you'll look stupid in front of everyone for speaking up.
- You stay in a job you hate because you're afraid you won't find another one.
- You buy the high-priced, one-year extended warranty on an inexpensive laptop because the salesperson said,

"If you don't buy the warranty, I'll be happy to sell you another laptop when you drop it, and it breaks during your next trip."

- You stay in a location you dislike because you're afraid to move to a new town without knowing anyone.
- You stay in a thirty-year marriage to a spouse who cheated several times because you fear being on your own.

Although these scenarios might not be one you fear, these are real-life situations from real people who have allowed fear to grip them. Fear shaped their decisions or their indecision, which is still a decision.

Power Buzz:
Dive Deeper into Fear

For a deeper dive into the causes of fear, read *The Big Leap* by Gary Hendricks, *Feel the Fear and Do It Anyway* by Susan Jeffers, Ph.D., or *Daring Greatly* by Brené Brown.

Game Changer:
Kick Fear Out

Fear has a positive side, too. Fear pushes you out of your comfort zone. Fear forces you to shift your thinking, to have faith over fear, and to move when your back is against the wall because you ran out of options. Fear can paralyze you or force you to change—your choice.

Implement these simple ways to kick fear out.

1. Blow bubbles. Use bubbles to reduce fear, stress, and negative emotions, suggests Laura Crooks, R.N., and Burnout Speaker and Coach. To make a bubble, you need a slow and steady breath. Making bubbles for one to two minutes can shift your nervous system and positively change your mood. Bubbles make you smile because it brings you back to childhood.

2. Imagine the worse. What is the worse that could happen? More than likely, the worse will never happen because your fear manifests extreme plans. Despite this, let's play out the worst-case scenario. Define it. After the truck incident, I imagined the worse—that I would be homeless.

3. Sit in your fear. You've defined your fear. When you sit in your fear, you explore alternative ways to handle your doubt. Play it out before it happens. Role-playing allows you to take control instead of letting the fear control you. You develop positive solutions to overcome your concerns. When I sat in the fear of being homeless, I knew it was my imagination creating the fear. My family and friends would offer a place until I could create an action plan, which is exactly what happened. When you sit in your fear, you're building resilience and your Bounce-Up Factor.

4. Create calm with meditation. Meditation eliminates distractions, helps you relax, and enables you to increase your focus. Download a free meditation with legendary renowned expert Louise Hay at LouiseHay.com. Or download a free app, such as Oak-Mediation & Breathing, Meditation Time, or Stop, Breathe, and Think. Devote five minutes or more of meditation to create calm.

5. Visit your happy place. You probably heard this one before and ignored it. This time do it. Picture a space or location that instantly shifts your mood. Is it the beach, a church, hiking trail, an amusement park, or some other favorite spot? When you feel fear sneaking in like those ants at your picnic, pause. Imagine standing in the middle of your happy place. Smile. Your goal is to slow down the panic associated with fear. When you replace shallow breathing and a racing heart rate caused by the danger felt, you enable positive thoughts and actions to form. A step needed to build your new resilience so that you can Bounce-Up.

Behind-the-Scene with Mj:
Visualize the Beach Escape

When I started the position with the builder, I craved a beach escape. Broke, living in Pittsburgh, PA, a city known for its gray days and murky rivers, it wasn't happening. That's when I chose to land in my happy place. I closed my eyes and imagined standing bare feet on a sun-kissed beach. The sand sifted into my toes. The sunrays warmed my face with the seagulls singing. The ocean salt tickled my nose as my shoulders relaxed. My tensed muscles melted like soft butter, and I was wearing a bikini built like a brick house. *Thirty-six, twenty-four, thirty-six, oh, she's a brick house...*

Okay, a gal can dream, right? Alright, I know this is a little cheesy. However, the point is to find your unique happy place.

Bounce-Up
Momentum

- Pinpoint your fear trigger(s).
- Complete Tip #2 and #3 under Game Changer: Kick Fear Out.
- Know how fear influences your decisions.
- Borrow fear-related books from your library.
- Buy bubbles to have on hand when fear or stress attacks.
- Start meditating.
- Create your Happy Place.

Boost Your Bounce-Up Factor:
Kick Fear Out

Understand how fear has influenced your life so that you can recognize the signals in the future.

1. How has fear shaped one of your decisions before?
2. What decision have you regretted because it was based in fear?
3. Do you identify with one of the examples?
4. What is one takeaway you gained from this chapter?
5. What is one positive action you will take?

Bounce-Up Wordology

Bounce-Up: Bouncing back to where you were before your setback can land you right back in the same place. Instead, *Bounce Up* higher and stronger than you were before the face-plant.

Sticky Monster Ball: An analogy used for the Fear roadblock. The sticky monster ball kid toy that kids can throw at the wall, and it grips the wall is the way fear can grip you.

CHAPTER 3
Verbal Drama Bounces Out-of-Control Like a Superball

"Mere words can help us overcome." **- Mjism**

Now that you know how to kick fear out the door, let's tackle the next roadblock: Verbal Drama. The drama that bounces around inside your mind ricocheting from one self-defeating thought to another resembles a superball that keeps going and going and going. Sometimes those self-defeating thoughts seem like they have a valid point, though most often, they're without any validation.

Think about bouncing a superball. Is it in control or out-of-control? In control when it's in your hand but as soon as it leaves your hand it's out-of-control. A superball bounces all over the place without any direction.

Consider mindset. Mindset can be positive or negative. When we direct our mindset, it's under control. As we let our mindset run wild, it's out of control. Mindset can influence or sabotage. Most sports teams have a player who hits the rink, field, or court to be an enforcer or intimidator. By talking trash or using strategic non-verbal communication, the intimidator gets into his opponent's head.

Verbal Drama Takes You Out of the Game
NFL cornerback Jalen Ramsey holds a title as one of the most relentless trash talkers in the National Football League. Jalen's trash-talking goal is to take his opponent out of his game. *You're trash; you won't catch a pass.* You might think that sounds

relatively weak, how could that talk intimidate a 300-pound football player? It works because Jalen's trash talking never stops. He keeps going and going and going like a three-year-old asking, "why."

Your Verbal Drama has the same goal to take you out of your game. Negative messages that continue bouncing around are probably the ones your mind created. Most often, these messages that get in your head are false. It's self-defeating talk. When you tell yourself junk or lies that get into your head, they limit or squash the action you will take to reach your goal. That pessimistic talk will keep you down. Somewhere in your subconscious, you know this.

The chatter in your head can deter you the way Jalen Ramsey's trash talk hinders his opponents, except your chatter is supposed to be on your team. That negative chatter creates one or more of the following positions.

- Blame game. It's everyone else's fault. "The customers were jerks." "Our prices are too high."
- Collison course. In your mind, you're heading down the path that will only result in a collision. You've manifested the current challenge into the worst-case scenario.
- Inner sabotage. You are critical of yourself or judge yourself, yet you would not be as demanding with friends.
- Victim outlook. Everything happens to you. It's the message playing in your head. "Why me?" "Why does everything happen to me?" "Why can't I get a break?"
- Word menace. Negative, self-defeating words and phrases are a significant part of your internal vocabulary. Specific words are like the neighborhood menace who wreaks havoc on everyone.

Power Buzz:
Brains Hardwired for Negativity

Our brains are hardwired to think negatively first, according to a study led by Jason Moser, a psychology professor at Michigan State University. Without a focus, our brains will drift to the negative.

Collision Course Example

During an entrepreneur conference I attended with a colleague, a presenter shared several simple conversation starters for networking. One of the suggestions included asking, "What's your favorite movie?" Sighing, my colleague said, "Why would someone tell me that?"

My colleague let his Verbal Drama take over. Why wouldn't someone share a favorite movie? People enjoy sharing their stories and information. My colleague went to the impossible before trying it.

Inner Sabotage Examples

One sales training client, an ambitious millennial financial planner, bombarded his potential clients with information. Enough information that could make a person feel like he had a truckload of manure dumped on him. The financial planner lost sale after sale. When we talked about it, he felt prospects wouldn't trust him because of his age. Trust is a huge issue when it comes to money, right? He wanted to show future clients how much he knew. This millennial's Verbal Drama created a scenario in his head that clients would focus on his age and wouldn't work with him. Once he shifted his inner dialogue, his conversations transformed. His book of business grew because he focused on his customers' needs. Two years later, he had his own independent office.

In the 1990s, Jose Lima was a star pitcher for the Houston Astros. In 1999, he won 21 games, was considered the best pitcher in the league and made the All-Star Team. In 2000, the team moved to what is currently called Minute Maid Park. (The park's history included names such as Enron Field and Astros Field until 2002 when the official name became Minute Maid Park.) The left field fence was much closer than the fence in the Astrodome, which favors the hitter, not pitchers.

Reportedly, the first time Jose Lima stood on the mound and looked at left field, he said, "I'll never be able to pitch in here. The fence is way too close."

Lima went from a 21-game winner to a 16-game loser. Verbal Drama? Disruption? Absolutely. The new field disrupted his mindset, which hurt his game.

Word Menace Examples

You allow negative thoughts to drive you right into the worst-case scenario. Marisa was downsized out of a job twice in four years. (Her name was changed to protect her privacy.) In her late 50s, she insisted she wouldn't get hired because she was too old. Who would hire her? Instead of focusing on her value and experience, she concentrated on her age.

One training client, let's call her Sierra, had the *I'm Not Syndrome*. In our first conversation, she shared, "I didn't go to college. This position relies on prospecting in the corporate sector. I don't know how to talk to corporate executives. I don't know what I was thinking taking this job."

Sometimes our brain sends a warning signal because it feels we're in danger. More than likely, Sierra felt uncomfortable in an environment she had little experience. So, Sierra concentrated on what she didn't have instead of what she had.

Recognize Truth or Verbal Drama, aka Head Trash

Sometimes, we *think* we know something isn't going to work because it doesn't make sense in our head. My conference-attending colleague fits this example.

Unless there's an acting background in your past, what's in your head, all that downbeat chatter, will show in your actions, intonation, and the words you use.

With preconceived ideas, we can't see opportunities. It's like going home the same way every day. We always do it this way. It's a habit.

Power Buzz:
Verbal Drama Knows No Boundaries

Verbal Drama impacts even the most successful people. Actor Christina Ricci portrayed more than 50 film and television characters. One would think with such success, the inner critic would skip Christina Ricci. Yet in several interviews, she shared that she covered all the mirrors in her house and couldn't have one in her bedroom because she hated herself.

Head talk impacts people in strange ways and can seize one's confidence, spirit, and potential. When we take control, we take the power away from Verbal Drama. We give ourselves power.

Shift Your Perspective

During an in-depth conversation about change with a colleague, licensed counselor Amy Toothman, I mentioned I use the word "shift" instead of "change" with my clients and during my keynote presentations. Shift doesn't seem to create as much resistance as the word "change" does. Amy ran with the idea.

"We need to shift the gears in our car if we want to reach a destination," Amy said, as her facial expressions brighten. "By shifting, it takes you where you want to go."

Exactly. The only way to overcome Verbal Drama is to shift your perspective. The best way to shift your attitude is to reflect on what you've achieved that boosts your confidence. (Stay tuned for your eye-opener and confidence booster with the Super-Size-You Activity in Chapter 5.)

In Marisa's example, she focused on her fear of not getting another job because of her age. When we sat down and worked through my Super-Size-You activity, she realized she had more to offer. Her accomplishments squashed her fear. Her mantra became *"My strength in communication enables me to work with high school students through the senior population. Communication is an asset in the HR department. I love to solve problems that others find frustrating."*

Success Bound:
Mj's Let Go Claw

You probably think this is the part where I talk about the overused phrase in conjunction with the mega-hit Disney tune sung by Idina Menzel as Elsa in the movie *Frozen*. Experts suggested the *let it go* theory in self-development long before the 2013 movie release, and there's another way to think about letting it go—*Mj's Let Go Claw*.

Visualize the vending game machine you'll find in arcades, shopping centers, and family restaurants. It's the game jammed with kid toys with a mechanical arm that moves back and forth until it drops the metal claw to grab a prize. Well, you hope the claw grabs something or else you're sinking additional dollar bills into that money slot, especially if you promised a toy to a little one.

Think of the toys as your baggage or challenge you get to dump into the trash, toilet, landfill, or God's hand. Now, let's eliminate what's keeping you stuck. Use the Let Go Claw to do it.

- Create a claw with your right hand.
- Hold your right arm up shoulder height with the claw hand facing the floor.
- Hold out your left arm to the side, hip height, with your left palm up toward the sky.
- Imagine your left palm is the dumpster, toilet, landfill, or God's hand. Imagine the baggage is in front of you.
- Take whatever challenge, setback, adversity, or baggage is weighing you down and grasp it with your claw hand.
- Slide your right hand, the claw hand, over top of your left hand, the dumpster, and let it go.

You dropped your baggage or challenge into the center of the dumpster. Done. Gone. Move on. Smile and relax.

Game Changer:
Drive Your Conversations

Moving your discouraging conversation to an encouraging one is like driving out of a cold, miserable foggy morning and into a beautiful, dazzling sunny afternoon. You can feel the warmth through your windshield, it's so much easier to drive, and it instantly brightens your day.

Now it's time for you to stop the chatter bouncing around your head like a superball.

1. Recognize Verbal Drama. What negative messages hold you hostage? Write them down.

2. Flip it. Flip the negative verbal drama to a positive verbal message. Flip any negative words into positive words. Negative phrases cause failure. Change the words in your head. For example, one night, I was driving home alone from my son's college basketball game. During the four-hour trip, a snowstorm started on a major highway known as a snowbelt. Whispering *please don't wreck, please don't wreck,* I realized wrecking held my attention. I flipped the words to *safe and sound.* For the next two hours, I chanted *safe and sound* over and over until I pulled onto my street.

3. Get a negativity alert. Ask others to nudge you when they hear the negative talk. One of my clients thought she was positive. Her co-workers didn't agree. It affected her job. She voiced more negative talk than positive. During one session, I mentioned that I would tap on the table any time I heard a negative statement to give her awareness. Then, she needed to flip the sentence to a positive one. To get in the positivity habit, she created a "Verbal Drama jar." With help from her co-workers and husband, anytime they heard a negative comment, my client had to put a quarter into the jar. Again, she'd flip her words into a positive comment.

4. Tame the Verbal Drama. Be on a mission to change your thoughts. If you're not driving toward a destination with a positive outcome, your negative thoughts will take over. When I was 16, I hopped onto my brother's minibike he left unattended in front of our house because dad wasn't home, yet. Even though I was a year older than my

brother, I wasn't allowed on it. (Yes. Dad had gender double standards.) Driving down our walkway to the sidewalk, I needed to make a sharp right turn to avoid hitting mom's car. Without realizing it, I steered the bike in the direction of my focus. You probably guessed what I did. Imagine a big gaping hole in mom's passenger door. I drove precisely where I focused my thoughts.

Bounce-Up
Momentum

- Identify your Verbal Drama. Is it Blame Game, Collision Course, Inner Sabotage, Victim Outlook, or Word Menace?
- Pinpoint inner chatter you say automatically.
- Use Flip It to convert negative talk into positive statements.
- Ask a family member or friend to give you a negativity alert.
- Focus on positive events.

Boost Your Bounce-Up Factor:
Eliminate Autopilot Statements

Our Verbal Drama becomes a habit like driving the same way home—autopilot.

1. Write down your daily "autopilot" statements. Simple examples include "I'm going to be late." "My boss always criticizes me." "I can't catch a break." "You don't know how difficult it is."

2. Take time right now to find another way to say it positively.
3. What other recurring Verbal Drama do you need to change?
4. What is one takeaway you gained from this chapter?
5. What is one positive action you will take?

Bounce-Up Wordology

Super-Size-You: An activity in Chapter 5 that enables you to discover the best version of you by completing three simple questions that pinpoint your core strengths you have buried under life's challenges.

Superball: An analogy used for the Verbal Drama roadblock. The negative chatter inside your head bounces out-of-control the way a superball bounces out-of-control.

Verbal Drama: The self-talk consisting of all the inner dialogue and drama about why you can't reach a goal or your potential. There's a dramatic story bouncing around inside your head giving an excuse why you can't do something. You've played the entire adverse scenario in your head.

CHAPTER 4
Immobilized Like a Hacky Sack That Hits the Floor

"One simple action rolls into the snowball effect." - **Mjism**

Now that you've waved good-bye to Fear and Verbal Drama, let's talk about the last roadblock: Immobility. Life has a way of throwing lemons at you—hard and fast. Sometimes, too hard and too fast to catch them. They knock you down. You become immobilized, and you can't get up. You could be tired of trying to solve the problem, tired of hitting that brick wall or tired of repeating the same pattern.

There are times that you're stuck because of the environment, economy, someone else's choice, or fate. You were in the wrong place during fate's spell. At times, the decisions you've made are the ones that land you where you are right now. Is your hand raised? Mine is.

When efforts lead to nowhere, you stop. Immobility is like a hacky sack that hit the floor. Or the problem occurs, and you think you don't have a choice, so you don't act. Being stagnant turns into a decision. You've chosen to stay in the same place.

Maybe, it's avoidance or hiding. Avoidance and hiding are cousins to Immobility. You hide or avoid the situation like Christina Wallace. When Christina's venture-backed clothing company Quincy Apparel failed, she spent three weeks in bed. After her company went bankrupt, Christina avoided the situation. Imagine, she didn't come out for three weeks, that's 21 days under the covers. If sinking into an Immobility Funk can happen to a rock star like Christina

37

Wallace, it can happen to anyone. You'll read more about how Christina moved out of her Immobility Funk and Bounced-Up in Chapter 6. In the meantime, let's not follow that Hacky Sack example.

Avoid iHunch, aka Text Neck

Immobility and avoidance can happen in your personal life and your professional life. Some salespeople will schedule non-revenue producing meetings to avoid going into the office when they know their sales are low. One accountant who had to address collections with customers would focus on spreadsheets, producing busy work rather than picking up the phone. Hiding behind digital devices keeps you stuck, too, and adds another issue researchers call "text neck" or "iHunch."

With iHunch, breathing slows down, shoulders roll in, neck and head tilt down, and your body appears smaller. This body language resembles the same presence as someone who suffers from clinical depression. Think about it. Our devices cause negative non-verbal communication and appearance.

A smaller body signals less confidence to our brains, as well as the way others look at us. What does this have to do with roadblocks? The more negativity in your body language, the fewer actions you will take. Fewer actions mean it takes longer for you to reach those goals, if ever. Are you prone to iHunch, seeming smaller, or what I call iBounce, your ability to reset your posture, appearing confident?

Success Bound:
Mj's Reset Button

In this easy-peasy two-minute activity called Mj's Reset Button, you'll drop the iHunch body language and reset your posture, so you'll look more in charge. With feet shoulder-width apart, clasp your hands together and stretch them over your head. In addition to the great feeling of the stretch, it opens your diaphragm, increases your breathing, and resets your shoulders, head, and neck into a favorable non-verbal position. As a bonus, while you're in your Reset position, say "I'm excited." The additional statement, "I'm excited," creates a positive mindset. Go!

Imagine being in a room of 1,500 people and everyone saying, "I'm excited" as they're standing in the Reset position. No one is in sync, and it's okay because this activity shifts the energy in the room, and it's fun. The next time you're in a meeting and your colleagues' concentration fades and shoulders slump have them stand up and engage in the Reset Button. You'll lead the shift of energy in the room.

Power Buzz:
"I'm Excited" Outperforms

Using three experiments, astute Harvard researchers found participants saying, "I am excited," before a high-stress-level activity felt more confident and outperformed the group that stated, "I am stressed," or, "calm down." When you think about it, saying "calm down" becomes a paradox.

Know Common Reasons for Immobility

Being stuck, immobilized stems from these common causes.

- Indecision. Unsure what action you must take, afraid of making the wrong decision, or expecting perfection, so you shut down. You stayed stuck in whatever rut you or someone else initiated. It's like stalling on an expressway ramp as your eyes dart from the rearview mirror to the merge lane ahead.

- Rearview Mirror. You can't shake rearview-mirror syndrome. Reliving over and over *what could have been* or *once was*. Or the *could've, should've and would've*. Living in the past is like going backward on a roller coaster. You're disoriented as the entire park zips past you, and you stop in the same place you started. Although a wild and crazy amusement park ride might be fun one day, it wouldn't be as much fun doing it every hour every day.

- Routine and Habits. Content with your current routines and habits because it's your comfort zone. Your actions are familiar. Familiarity breeds compliant people. You might not be in the best place, but you're not in the worst situation, so why change. You're doing the same thing repeatedly, professionally, or personally. You're on a treadmill to nowhere.

- The Problem. You're engrossed in the problem. The problem captivates your mind and body. With a tunnel-vision focus on the issue, you can't shift to the solution.

Negative Emotions Stick

"I'm at a Chamber networking meeting. I ran into a broker I have staged for one of her listings. The listing sold in three weeks. She made money from my staging! She has another vacant house, and it isn't selling. She told me she's going to stage it herself. That's like me saying to her, 'Oh yeah, I have a neighbor who is trying to sell her house, but I'm going to tell her to sell it herself.' Sorry, but I'm over these realtors," texted a colleague who is a home stager. To protect her privacy, let's call her Stormie Stuck.

Stormie's emotions played the main character in her text. Upset and angry, she could only focus on the statement that the former client made. Another piece to this dilemma—it wasn't the first time a realtor or broker felt she could stage the house herself, whereas Stormie is a professional stager with years of experience.

"Did you remind her that her last vacancy sold within three weeks of you staging it?" I asked.

"No," she admitted.

"Did you ask her how often she staged a listing?"

"No."

"Did you mention the top two mistakes homeowners and realtors make when they try to stage a home themselves?"

"No."

Stormie stayed stuck in the whirlwind of negative emotions that surfaced every time a similar situation occurred. Rather than educate the person, the home stager dug into her annoyance. She couldn't think. Stormie couldn't respond. She couldn't let it go. She couldn't move forward.

"Create a tip sheet," I texted. "List the top five mistakes homeowners and realtors make when they try to stage a house themselves."

An hour later, I received a message from Stormie. "I finished writing the five mistakes sellers and realtors make when staging houses themselves. It only took me five short minutes. Thanks."

Watch for Signals

I post regularly on LinkedIn as a simple way to share messages that relate to my speaking and training business. Sometimes, I tackle resilience topics, and sometimes I cover sales topics. In the spring of 2019, I posted the following message tackling resilience.

You never think it will happen to you, yet it does. You didn't get the coveted promotion. You lost the biggest sale of the year. Your critique group hated your children's fiction manuscript. Those might not be the setbacks that happened to you.

All three of those setbacks and many, many more have happened to me. Sometime when you want to kill an hour or two, let's have coffee. I digress. After each setback, I reflected and reevaluated. I asked questions. I sought advice. I let go of the loss. I shifted direction.

What happened? Each setback came with a new opportunity. A recruiter from another company offered a better position with a higher salary. A former client referred two of his colleagues who became clients. A consumer magazine bought and published one of my non-fiction articles, which later lead to a book contract. A pivot happened with each setback. Each setback offered an opportunity to Bounce-Up—higher and stronger than before.

Go ahead and welcome your next setback! What pivot do you need to make? How will you Bounce-Up?

After that post, I received a private message from Jennifer, someone I didn't know. Here's her note.

"This past Monday I was unjustly fired (and while it's what comes from most people that do get fired, this termination was corrupt). I have only had one other job that I left unprepared for the next job—didn't have anything lined up but took a complete

step of faith—that was 10 years ago. At that time, I made it my job to find a job. A single mother at the time, I took my son to daycare and took my resume out, filled out applications, interviewed, and kept my mind open to all options. After two weeks, I got a call, offering me a position I had not even applied for [by the same woman who fired me]. That step propelled my career in ways I never imagined. I was fired 12/31/18 and had been struggling to get my mindset back to where I was then [10 years ago]. To welcome this opportunity, to embrace the change that will be, and for opportunities that match my abilities. I know I will get there - and it's because of your article that I need to read over and over and process what just happened—something goodwill present, and I welcome this 'setback.' From my heart, I thank YOU—for what you do."

Jennifer shared her struggle, which kept her stagnant. She couldn't get past the circumstances that would enable her to move forward. Jennifer needed to get unstuck. To look at her current situation so that she could become the determined goal-oriented businesswoman she was 10 years earlier.

For her, she received the right message that offered the encouragement she needed to hear at the right time that would shift her perspective. She Bounced-Up once; she could do it again.

Jennifer's Update: She is now an executive director for a non-profit organization.

Toss the Dirt Like Aaron Judge

New York Yankees right fielder Aaron Judge uses a similar method of tossing negative thoughts. When he starts beating himself up mentally during an at-bat, he steps out of the box, picks up some dirt, crushes it, and once the Yankee's right fielder finishes crushing it, he throws the dirt away. He imagines he's tossing his negative thoughts.

Action Needed. Apply Within.

Without action, a hacky sack can't get off the ground. Only movement can get you out of your Immobility Funk. Here's the deal. Being immobilized feels bad. Ignoring this feeling won't go away. That Immobility Funk stays with you until you deal with it. You deserve more.

Take the first baby step toward momentum. Each baby step forward feels good because you tackled that one step and moved forward. You accomplished it. Each action builds traction. Think of going down a slide. You give a little push off the top, and as you slide, you pick up speed. That same tiny step propels you away from passiveness and toward your goal, a promotion, a new career, an adventurous life, a stronger you, or whatever you wish.

Success Bound:
Make It Happen

- Got 15? Schedule at least 15 minutes, more if you can, to start one action.
- Write it. Decide what action you will take and write it down. Writing it down initiates making it happen. If you can't figure it out yourself, look at your Power Team for help. (See Tip #1 below under Game Changer.)
- Create it. Once you've established your action, create your affirmation. "I will _____." (Fill in the blank.) Write it on a notecard and post it. Turn your affirmation

and favorite photo into a meme with Canva.com or the Word Swag app.

- Do it. Don't think about doing it because you'll let your feelings get in your way. As the famous sports footwear and apparel company says, "just do it."
- Need ideas? Visit www.MjCallaway.com/BounceUp to get examples.

Power Buzz:
5-Second Blastoff

In her book, *The 5 Second Rule*, Mel Robbins suggests counting, "5-4-3-2-1," then start walking toward whatever idea your brain produced. Use her same counting system; direct your actions toward your decision. "5-4-3-2-1" move into action.

Game Changer:
Create Your Momentum

1. Build your Power Team. This group of people will be your support team. Family members, friends, colleagues, and mentors who can listen, guide you, offer advice or suggestions, provide a smiling face, and calming tone. The people who will be honest with you in a diplomatic way. The people who will be your champions. You can have a different Power Team for different goals. When working for the national builder, my Power Team included the General Manager Gary Young who taught me about land prep, walkout basements, and trusses; my friends Andrea and Tommy Hart who worked in the industry and gave advice about rough plumbing, kitchen layouts, and flooring; my co-worker Tom Saxton who showed me how

to read blueprints; and friend Tom Allen who once worked in construction and answered a ton of questions. Even superheroes have a Power Team, think about the movie *The Avengers: Endgame*. Want a few suggestions to build your Power Team? Go to www.MjCallaway.com/BounceUp to get your pre-made outline.

2. Get expert guidance. A business consultant, life or wellness coach, spiritual leader, or counselor can guide you in specific areas related to their expertise. Know what you need before you inquire about designated services. Do you need one-on-one time, or will a group environment work for you? **What outcome do you want to achieve?** Does the expert have experience obtaining the results you want with his or her clients?

3. Walk toward a purpose. Each step moves you away from immobility and gives you momentum toward your desired outcome. Small steps convert into more significant actions. Think of driving to a fun destination. Each mile marker you reach takes you closer to your location. After holding my first co-authored book project for five months, McGraw-Hill passed on it because we didn't have enough of an author's platform. We jumped into action. The first action was to find out what the publishing house wanted when it came to an author's platform. Next, we created a marketing plan and reached out to website owners, organizations, and women's groups that fit our target audience. Four months later, Warner Books, now Grand Central Publishing, offered a contract for *The Frantic Woman's Guide to Life* and a year later a deal for *The Frantic Woman's Guide to Feeding Family and Friends* written under my pen name. What is the outcome you want? What is the first action you can take?

4. Tie purpose with pleasure. Wrap together a commitment with a fun activity. The fun activity can be a big thing or a little thing. It can be listening to an author's reading, or it could be a special dinner. In the middle of writing this book, I was stuck. [Pun intended.] I booked a hotel room in a charming village for three days. Making this commitment forced me to write the chapters I had put off because if I didn't produce, I would've wasted the money I spent on the hotel room and travel. Money that I could've earmarked for another business expense. On the day I checked out, I meandered around the village, ate lunch, and enjoyed a beautiful spring day.

Despite the event(s) that happened to you, you can shape the outcome. You can influence it with your actions and your mindset.

Bounce-Up
Momentum

- Implement the Reset Button when needed.
- Pinpoint the reason you are stuck.
- Use Mj's Let Go Claw to flush out the negativity keeping you down.
- Use pro player Aaron Judge's Toss the Dirt method to move on.
- Build your Power Team.
- Get expert guidance in the specific area you need help.
- Create a purpose and walk toward it.

**Boost Your Bounce-Up Factor:
Move It!**

1. What has caused you to be stuck?
2. How long have you felt like you were in the same place or not moving forward as fast as you'd like?
3. What outside resources can help you build momentum?
4. What is one takeaway you gained from this chapter?
5. What is one positive action you will take?

Bounce-Up Wordology

Hacky Sack: An analogy used for the Immobility roadblock. Without action, a hacky sack doesn't move; it's immobilized.

iBounce: Your ability to reset your posture, appearing confident.

iHunch: When using digital devices, your breathing slows down, shoulders roll in, neck and head tilt down, and the body seems smaller. Also, it can be called text neck.

Immobilized: You remain stuck in the same spot as a hacky sack without action.

Immobility Funk: You want to stick your head in the sand and not come out because maybe the situation will go away.

Part II

Bounce-Up™ Fundamentals

CHAPTER 5
Unshakability Creates the Foundation

You bounced back before; you can
bounce-up this time! - **Mjism**

Now it's time to talk about the fundamentals to help you Bounce-Up. The first fundamental you need is Unshakability. Unshakable when challenges occur. Unshakable in your belief to overcome adversity. Unshakable in your abilities to meet challenges head-on.

Originally, this chapter's theme was "self-efficacy." I loved the definition of the word and it embodied the meaning and theme of this chapter. Self-efficacy signifies your belief in your abilities, and your ability to meet challenges head-on.

Behind-the-Scene with Mj:
Instinct Overrules Stubbornness

A little detour here—sometimes I can be a little bit stubborn. Ask my family. I get something in my head, and I plow full-steam ahead. I hear the well-intended chatter, yet I ignore it. You're probably wondering what my stubbornness has to do with Unshakability and self-efficacy. When I was writing my keynote, *Bounce-Up During Disruptions*, the inspiration for this book, my Tri-State Mastermind power women suggested I use a different word. My friend, colleague, and Co-President of National Speakers Association Pittsburgh Chapter Bob Pacanovsky made me explain what it meant. I did get it, especially when you're saying "self-efficacy" from the stage in front of a thousand people without the word written out on a screen. It's one of those 10th grade words according to Readability formulas and let's be upfront, who uses self-efficacy in daily life.

The signs were there to eliminate it. When the CEO of a billion-dollar company asked me to explain the meaning of self-efficacy, the fingers of doubt plowed in like a steam roller. I ignored them...until the final edits of this book. Replacement words rolled around inside my head. On the way to a speaking engagement, using my car's Bluetooth, I called Bob. "What do you think of the word unshakable instead of self-efficacy?"

Laughter echoed inside the car. "I can't believe you're even asking **me** that question because you know **my** answer," Bob barely got out in between his laughter. "Even the word 'crayon' would be better than self-efficacy."

"Crayon? Crayon!!"

On a lighter side, if you want to impress others during a meeting or party, tell someone they have self-efficacy. They'll look at you with a blank stare. Then, you can explain the meaning and get a round of "ohs." Maybe you'll get that promotion you wanted.

Be Unshakable

With days before this book hit my editor's desk, my instinct told me replacing the word was the right move. I love the power of the word *unshakable*. It's a word I've use often, which is the reason I overlooked it. Unshakable implies significance, spirit, and belief. Your strengths become your Unshakability.

This one word signifies your belief in your abilities, and your ability to meet challenges head-on. Your determination that you will succeed. When Unshakability seeps from your soul, you're more likely to recover after adversity, disruptions, or a failure because you leverage your abilities to overcome any setbacks you encounter. Harnessing your talents and strengths develops an unshakable attitude.

With Unshakability, you forget the naysayers because their opinions don't matter to you. You say, "I got what it takes." You believe you have influence and control over your life. Being unshakable provides the trust you need in your ability to get up after life's faceplants, leverage your strengths, create an action plan, and achieve your designated goal.

Assess Your Abilities

To become unshakable, eliminate as many of the negative distractions that absorb your attention. Avoid taking on someone else's burdens. It's time to focus on your abilities. Maybe you're groaning right now at that statement.

Work, family responsibilities, and current events happening in your life steal your attention and your time. Today's circumstances might not be ideal for you. You might not be where you want to be at this stage in your life. Maybe you have little available time between your commitments, or you don't feel you can take the time for yourself—time you need to look at your abilities and what you achieved in your own life.

More than likely, you haven't taken the time to pause, reflect, and assess. Without breaking from your day-to-day responsibilities to assess your abilities, you can't build an action plan. Nor can you implement habits you need for your action plan to work. You can't ask and get help. You can't gain momentum.

Block out time to assess your abilities so that you can leverage those skills for your future. By evaluating those talents, you'll feel encouraged to be unshakable.

Pull some inspiration from a child's playbook. Children are resilient, and they adapt faster than adults. Roadblocks wouldn't stop kids when it comes to getting what they want and having fun. As basic as it sounds, when you were learning to walk, you bounced up each time you tumbled. You have everything in YOU to Bounce-Up.

Shoot for Unshakable Belief

At two years old, Josh Rulnick started ice skating, and by age five, he played on a mini-mite hockey team. Before Josh hit six, doctors diagnosed him with Perthes' disease, which deteriorates the hip ball joint. For the next seven years, the doctor restricted Josh from running, hopping, skipping, and jumping. All the actions of a typical elementary-aged child. Imagine keeping your child or a friend's child from running, hopping, skipping, or jumping. When the doctor diagnosed Josh, the doctor told Josh and his parents that his one leg would be shorter than the other, he wouldn't be very tall, and he wouldn't be good in sports.

Fast forward to Josh's senior year at LaRoche College (now LaRoche University). His Division III basketball team played against the Division I Pitt Panthers in an exhibition game at Peterson Event Center in Pittsburgh, Pennsylvania. Josh dribbled down the court for a layup going against 6' 8" Sam Young, who would be drafted by the Memphis Grizzlies, and 6' 8" DeJuan Blair, who would be selected by San Antonio Spurs.

At 5' 7"—yes, an entire foot shorter than the two Pitt players—Josh demonstrated Unshakability. His belief in his ability regardless of what the doctor predicted, the odds against him with two guards defending the ball.

During Josh's college basketball career, he used his speed, driving to the hoop or driving to the corner for an outside shot. As most of the players towered over him, he got fouled frequently; an advantage for him and his team, as he consistently made his free throw shots. For five years after Josh graduated college, he held the school record for the most consecutive free throw shots.

Success Bound:
Super-Size-You Powers

Your strengths form your foundation for Unshakability. This simple, yet insightful activity, Super-Size-You Powers, is one I developed when I started over and needed to find a position that offered more income to rebuild my life and get my son through college. After finishing this activity, I uncovered strengths that became my core foundation. These skills and strengths were my assets as I moved forward.

You will determine the strengths, characteristics, traits, and resources you've utilized previously to overcome setbacks or accomplish a goal. Once you identify your Super-Size-You Powers, you will be able to leverage them to increase your Bounce-Up Factor. In the example below, I've used the outcome of one of my clients as a guide. You can download this activity at www.MjCallaway.com/BounceUp.

A. List two to three accomplishments. Think of your life and write down two to three achievements you're proud of obtaining. (Psst. You can list all of your accomplishments, then choose your top two.)

Marisa's example: She had 25 years' experience as an HR Executive
1.
2.
3.

B. What did it take to achieve it? Think about your skills, actions, characteristics, talents, strengths, and so forth. These are your Super-Size-You Powers. Examples include courage, creativity, discipline, and resourcefulness.
Marisa's examples: Tenacity, problem-solver, tackles deadlines with a plan, handles extreme pressure, communicates well with all ages, empathic, patient.
1.
2.
3.
4.
5.

C. What challenges did you face while reaching your achievements? (The results you noted above.) Examples include putting yourself through college while holding down a job, working your way up the corporate leader, turning a side hustle into a business, running a marathon, surviving an illness, or relocating to a new city by yourself without knowing anyone. Marisa's examples: During one HR position, the company merged with another, and Marisa was responsible for breaking the news, walking employees through the exit interviews, and handling all the benefits and severance packages.
1.
2.
3.

D. Consider how your Super-Size-You Powers help you Bounce-Up, create significant habits, and reach your goals.

Super-Size-You Powers	I will use my Super-Size-You Powers to:

Superpowers Form Your Foundation

Once you have finished your Super-Size-You activity, make these *superpowers* form your foundation. You have that foundation within you, only it's buried under all the distractions, setbacks, and baggage dumped on you and your foundation over the years. Your Super-Size-You Powers proves you can do it. You did it once. You have what it takes to reach your achievements. The same traits and behaviors you can use as your foundational belief to be unshakable.

Sure, there's a possibility that the odds are against you right now in whatever adversity you might face. The same way the odds were against five-year-old Josh. You influence whether you see it as a risk or opportunity.

Before you deliberate, look at your Super-Size-You Powers. You bounced back before; now it's time to believe you can **Bounce-Up!**

Power Buzz:
What's Your Brand?

What does your brand say about you? A brand identifies you. It's the impression you give to others and the way others see you through your actions and communication. You have a brand personally and professionally, and they need to be congruent. When you aren't congruent with your brand, you're off-kilter. You can self-manage your brand, too. Take a short, complimentary self-brand assessment at www.selfbrand.com.

Game Changer:
Tap into Your Unshakability

Now that you've pinpointed your Super-Size-You Powers, here is a step-by-step action plan to build Unshakability.

1. Word it out. Create your manifesto by putting your Super-Size-You keywords into a word cloud creator, such as https://worditout.com/word-cloud/create. Post it in critical places where you can see it regularly.

2. Think opportunity. View your situation as an opportunity. Every time a negative thought surfaces, stop the negativity from going any further. Remember *Flip It* from Chapter 3. After you flip it to a positive thought, create a chant. "I get an opportunity to grow. I get an opportunity to find a better solution."

3. Persist in the journey. Keep looking for a solution. "What can I do today with what I have?" Write this question on an index card or Post-It note and hang it as a reminder.

4. Create alternate options. Make it a game by brainstorming as many alternative options as possible. It doesn't matter if you think they're impossible. The only goal here is to create more ideas. You might find one that sounds crazy and doable. Ask your Power Team (introduced in Chapter 4) to brainstorm options.

5. Set yourself up for success. Each step becomes a brick in the success path. As you achieve each level, write down the accomplishment. Each victory adds another block to your success and self-efficacy foundation. When I decided to obtain women-owned business certification by Women's Business Enterprise National Council (WBENC), the daunting application caused an immediate "Are you

kidding me?" The required documents brought back memories of filling out the FAFSA forms when my kids went to college. To overcome the intimidating task, I printed out the three-page list of mandatory documents and attached them to my magnetic board. Breaking the requirements into bite-size chunks, I checked off what I had finished, making it a doable goal.

6. Be your own cheerleader. Cheer for each step that moves you forward. Give yourself kudos for every single step, regardless of the size you achieve. You did it. You moved forward. Reward yourself for completing the goal. One colleague, author and business owner Rita Bergstein, treats herself like her best employee. Rita says, "I buy myself something so that every time I use it; I think of my success. I walked myself into Louis Vuitton on Fifth Avenue in New York City and splurged." Here are a few suggestions from my colleagues.

Intangible
- Have a "Me" day
- Look in the mirror and say, "you did it"
- Smile and take another step
- Share with others to encourage them
- Enjoy an evening sunset
- Sit with the accomplishment

Tangible
- Enjoy an adult beverage
- Plan a special meal out with family or friends
- Invest in an electronic gadget
- Read a new book
- Schedule a trip
- Buy a piece of jewelry

Bounce-Up Momentum:

- Complete the Super-Size-You activity.
- Assess your abilities, aka, your superpowers after completing Super-Size-You.
- Generate your manifesto or word cloud with your Super-Size-You superpowers.
- Take the SelfBrand assessment.
- Think opportunities.
- Consistently ask yourself, *What can I do today with what I have?*
- Be your own cheerleader.
- Set yourself up for success with an achievable to-do list.
- Reward yourself.

Boost Your Bounce-Up Factor: Build Your Ability Foundation

1. What achievement did you discover that you had forgotten?
2. Did you see common traits that can boost your Unshakability?
3. What strengths will help create strategies to achieve a new goal?
4. What is one takeaway you gained from this chapter?
5. What is one positive action you will take?

Bounce-Up Wordology

Self-Efficacy: Belief in your abilities, and determination for success. Leverage your strengths to overcome any setbacks you encounter.

Super-Size-You: Characteristics, strengths, talents, and traits that you have developed over the years. Consider them as your superpowers.

Unshakability: An unshakable belief in your strengths, ability, and determination to Bounce-Up. To leverage your strengths to accomplish a goal regardless of the adversity.

CHAPTER 6
Improvise to Spark Momentum

When you improvise, you improve your life. **- Mjism**

The second essential fundamental to Bounce-Up is Improvise. Trying to be perfect during adversity can stop you from overcoming a setback because you're looking for the perfect solution, scenario, or game plan. Although perfection would be fabulous, it's truly unrealistic. In the meantime, while you're waiting, you allow circumstances to rule you or you adapt to the situation. Then, you lose control because you've given the event or the situation control over the solution and sometimes over your life.

Adapting could stop you from improving. The word adapt means to make "fit." Would you rather "fit" yourself to the disruption? Or would you rather have some say in the situation? You want a say, right?!

When you Improvise, you take charge. You're resourceful.
- You ignite the opportunity to understand where you stand within the situation.
- You ignite the opportunity to seek support through your Power Team you gathered in Chapter 4.
- You ignite the opportunity to ask: *What can I do right now with what I have?*

Jumpstart improvisation by asking a Momentum Question, such as *What can I do right now with what I have?* Your brain focuses on answers, which creates action. Another

Momentum Question is *What solution can I create within the perimeter I have?*

Momentum Questions give you an active role in the outcome of the situation. Although I don't know your current circumstances, I understand it could be devasting. It could hurt worse than anything you've ever gone through before. I'm not glossing over the emotional turbulence that could be happening right now. What I know is focusing on that turbulence, reliving the actions that led to the setback, will deter you from building momentum and moving forward.

Asking the Momentum Question provides the segue for a new perspective. See a different viewpoint from a different angle. Once you start asking yourself Momentum Questions, the ones I offer or create your own, your focus shifts. You walk away from being a victim to be an ignitor, an action-taker.

Behind-the-Scene with Mj:
Change Momentum Questions

I mentioned how I started over with $500 when my safety was threatened. During the transitional time, I spent weeks reliving the event. This was the same timeframe that I went to work for the on-site builder, and all the disruptions of leaving my home that guests always said felt so welcoming when they visited and the community I loved. I'll admit a lot of Verbal Drama replayed and maybe a little bit of revenge occurred in that negative reminiscing as I slept on the sofa at my girlfriend's house until I could pull the resources together to rent an apartment. I wouldn't be human if those emotions hadn't occured. At the time, I thought, why was I paying the price. In reality, anyone suffering from an addiction paid a bigger price.

At an Al-Anon Conference, I learned the tactic *get busy, get better*. (This was also the time I created the Let Go Claw.) My biggest game-changer came through an off-handed comment I overheard. *The best revenge is a good life.* I recognize revenge thoughts played a part because I was on the sofa and my former spouse was in the welcoming house. Why was I giving away my time and power to past events? I made **the choice** to leave. Once I recognized those thoughts, my focus changed. I was done thinking about what I couldn't change. I flipped the not-so-good thoughts to "Life is Good" and implemented these Momentum Questions:

- What do I need to shift to make more money?
- How can I reinvent my life?
- What do I need to do to rebuild a better life for myself and my kids?
- How can I create a "life is good" life?

My motto became *Done. Gone. Move on.* I was **done** with the "what if" verbiage.

The need for revenge was **gone**, and it was time to **move on** because I was alive.

Power Buzz:
Impact of Alcohol Use Disorder

Sadly, more than 17.6 million people suffer from Alcohol Use Disorder (AUD) in the United States, according to the Centers for Disease Control and Prevention. University of Michigan researchers found that 50 percent of couples divorce when one partner has a history of alcoholism.

Behind-the-Scene with Mj:
A Gorgeous Improvisation

Only six years after the first life-altering event, and two years into my entrepreneurial journey, the second crisis occurred in late October of 2016. I received a cancer diagnosis. If chemotherapy didn't work—it had a 50 percent chance of working—I had a 20 percent chance of survival over the next five years. During the intensity of chemotherapy (imagine seven hours in a chair hooked up to an IV), which I called Magic Wand because it sounded so much better, it was the middle of a Pittsburgh winter. Visualize snow, freezing temperatures, and icy roads. Did I say snow? The integrative doctor suggested finding a way to walk more. Going to a gym was out of the question because it was a horrible flu season, and my immune system tanked. Catching a cold, flu, or virus would've granted me an express ticket to the hospital. The Monopoly game comes to mind. Go straight to jail, aka, the hospital.

What other options did I have? At first, I became a mall walker. Then, seeing an ad for Phipps Conservatory, I realized I had another option—to join the Conservatory. Walking around the Conservatory gave me a beautiful view, and a membership allowed unlimited visits. With seats placed throughout, I could sit and rest when my energy dropped. A simple improvisation provided so many benefits. The gorgeous surroundings uplifted my spirits, the exercise pushed the drugs through my body, the space provided a warm and safe environment, and plants gave off oxygen. Plus, the Conservatory has a wonderful café where I could work, too. I would stash my work bag in one of the lockers until after my walk.

Lemonade Starts a Movement

Before her first birthday, the doctors diagnosed Alexandra Scott with childhood cancer. At four, Alex wanted to raise money for what she considered "her hospital" so that "her doctors" could help other kids like her. With one idea, this brave little girl created a fundraiser using common kitchen ingredients to make lemonade. Her first lemonade stand raised $2,000. As Alex continued her efforts, other families joined her mission, and Alex's Lemonade Stands popped up in neighborhoods across the country. Before Alex passed away at age eight, her fundraising efforts, along with Lemonade Stand followers who heard about her mission, raised 1 million dollars. Alex's parents continued the momentum Alex started, which has now generated more than 80 million dollars. Incredible when you think about it. Alex's Lemonade Stand began with one action of one little four-year-old girl who had one idea.

Power Buzz:
Preschoolers Outwit College Kids!

Researchers gave preschoolers and college students the task of turning on an experimental music box using shapes. In the Blicket Experiment from the University of California, Berkeley, and the University of Edinburgh, they noted preschool children found more approaches to making the music box work than the college students. While the college kids stuck to the obvious approaches unsuccessfully, the preschoolers were open to improvising.

TV Series Spurs a Career Path

Bryan W. found himself with less work as a driver's education teacher because the public schools that once offered this subject as an elective now only offered it as an after-school program in his hometown. After seven years of trying to get a full-time position, Bryan found an unexpected idea while watching *Unbreakable Kimmy Schmidt,* co-created by the one and only Tina Fey. The title character, unemployed Kimmy, tries to make some money using an online and mobile marketplace called TaskRabbit.

At first, the teacher figured it was an imaginary company created for the show. Curiosity got the better of Bryan, and he checked the internet. Sure enough, TaskRabbit existed. TaskRabbit pairs freelance subcontractors to homeowners who need home repairs, furniture assembly, and other tasks. Bryan applied. He works for himself, though has the insurance, liability, operation, scheduling, invoicing, and payment collection of being an entrepreneur through a more significant entity with TaskRabbit.

Two years later, with more than 600 completed tasks, Bryan turned his simple search into a full-time career, specializing in mounting pictures and building IKEA furniture. Though the former teacher could've stayed stuck for another seven years waiting for a teaching position, Bryan heard an idea and asked what became his Momentum Question, "Does this exist?"

Success Bound:
Find Your Rhythm

People who Improvise Bounce Up higher and stronger than those who do not. Now, if you're a newbie at improvising, congratulations. You're on the right track. Keep going. Build your momentum. If you're on the "Improvise track" already, you can boost your Bounce-Up Factor by incorporating these Momentum Questions into your daily practices.

- What do I have right now that I can use?
- What resources can I pull?
- How would my Power Team solve this challenge?

End with an Unshakable statement.

- I will figure it out.

Turn I Can't into I Can

When one of Mary Maroadi's corporate clients needed a transport truck with electrical capabilities, her location specialist contacted trucking companies throughout the United States to find one Maroadi Transfer and Storage could rent. The specialist came up empty-handed in the search. The only truck known to handle this requirement was on the west coast and unavailable.

As president of the company, that fruitless search didn't stop Mary from brainstorming options with her mechanic. Refusing to tell a long-term client, "No, we can't do it," Mary's focus became, "How can we make this happen?" Two weeks later, with a bit of ingenuity, a custom-built generator, and mechanical engineering from her highly-skilled mechanic, Maroadi Transfer and Storage had a specialty truck to handle the job.

70 Conversations Jumpstarts a Career

Let's go back to Christina Wallace's failure with Quincy Apparel introduced in Chapter 4. When Christina realized she had to pay rent after spending several weeks burying her head under the covers, she knew she needed to seek opportunities. To get out of her Immobility Mode (my wordology, not hers), Christina invited people she knew in the New York City area to coffee. She arranged 70 coffee conversations over 30 days. Yes, that's a lot of coffee in a short amount of time. Christina had a mission. Over coffee, she asked three questions:

1. What do you come to me for help with?
2. When have you seen me happiest?
3. Where do I stand out against my peers?

These three questions were Christina's Momentum Questions. The responses gave her a clear vision of her strengths and what made her happy. This information became her Bounce-Up Factor. Christina improvised by using her resources, her network of people, and her questions, to create a future that would fit her best. The outcome: she received 7.5 million dollars in funding from the Helen Gurley Brown Trust for a STEM start-up. Currently, Christina is the Vice President of Growth at Bionic.

One conversation, or 70, can propel you into the livelihood you love. Be forewarned. Your "Improvise" conversations are not for you to play the victim. Remember, done, gone, and move on. The discussions are meant to propel you into action. It's a conversation or two with one BIG goal, and that is for you to Bounce-Up. When you follow Christiana's example, go into the discussion with an outcome in mind.

Here are four results you can gain:
- To move you from where you are right now to where you could be.
- To create options to solve the challenge.
- To gain a new positive perspective about the situation.
- To see a new opportunity.

Game Changer:
Momentum Builders

1. Apply the 30-second hello. Borrowing the 30-second hello action that I came across in the hospitality industry, it's a simple activity to jumpstart movement. As you see someone, whether you're out shopping or inside your workplace, say hello within 30 seconds. This simple act gets you out of your comfort zone and forces you to be impulsive, especially if you like to keep to yourself.
2. Join an Improv class or Toastmasters Club. While the Improv class's primary focus will be on improvisation, Toastmasters has a meeting segment called Table Topics, which will be off-the-cuff. Speaking off-the-cuff builds your improvising skillset muscle.
3. Convert a bad situation into a good one. Stanford University professor Tina Seelig's students create a list of great restaurant ideas and a list of lousy restaurant ideas. She divides the bad restaurant ideas among the

students, and they need to convert a bad idea into a good one. Professor Seelig shares this idea in her TED Talk "How to Catch Luck." What an ingenious way to foster improvisation. To Bounce-Up, follow Professor Seelig's example, and convert a bad situation into a good one.

4. Take a risk a day. If you're not an adventurous person, grab a friend and rent a kayak, canoe, or paddleboard for 30 minutes or an hour. Go ziplining. Visit a local state park, get a trail map, and hike. Pack up your laptop, current reading material, or hobby (if it's travel-friendly) and head to a coffee shop. Join a Meetup group, take a non-credit class, start a new pastime like playing the guitar you always wanted to try. Take a tour by yourself. Do something that makes your stomach topsy-turvy.

5. Replace "No" with "Yes, and." Instead of automatically saying *no*, replace it with *Yes, and,* a popular sales strategy and improv technique. By saying *Yes, and,* you get the opportunity to think about the ask, request, or inquiry.

6. Pay it forward. Do something unexpected and kind for someone else. By doing so, you can change your outlook as you bless someone else. In Grove City, Pennsylvania, there's this charming coffee shop called Beans on Broad with a chalkboard at the front entrance. Visitors check the chalkboard for their names. If it's there, they'll find a drink name, too. Someone paid it forward by treating them to a delightful beverage. How much fun would it be to see your name on the board? Being the one to pay it forward, how rewarding would it be to know you paid for that drink.

Bounce-Up Momentum

- Schedule conversations with positive people from your organization, church, and social networks.
- Create the Momentum Questions that will push you to Improvise.
- With your Super-Size-You Powers in mind, ask your network how they see you using your superpowers.
- Plan your coffee and conversations with people in your social and professional circles.
- Generate a list of solutions. Then, add five additional solutions. Creating other solutions will make you brainstorm beyond the typical outcomes.

Boost Your Bounce-Up Factor: Your Coffee Conversation Questions

Design your coffee and conversation movement. Figure out what questions you need to ask others to build your personal or professional movement. Use your desired outcome as the basis for your questions. Or use the first three questions below to get feedback from your Power Team, mentors, friends, and colleagues. Go!

1. What do you see as my super strength or assets?
2. What comes naturally to me?
3. What opportunities could I be overlooking?
4. What is one takeaway you gained from this chapter?
5. What is one positive action you will take?

Bounce-Up Wordology

Ignitor: A person who ignites action, an action-taker.

Immobility Mode: The inability to get out of your current situation so that you can move forward.

Momentum Question: A question you ask yourself to initiate brainstorming and provide the kick in the butt you need to get moving.

CHAPTER 7
Conviction Drives Success

Your belief in yourself drives your determination. - **Mjism**

The third critical fundamental to bouncing-up during adversity, disruptions, or setbacks is your Conviction. Conviction propels your actions, thoughts, and goals. Dogma drives your persistence and perseverance. Without Conviction, it's too easy to say another day. Without that steadfast belief, you will find yourself in the same place next year, the following year, and possibly ten years down the road. Sounds unbelievable, though true.

One resident came from a long line of doctors in the family. With some hesitation and unsure if he wanted to be a doctor, he followed the expected career path. Thirteen years later, in his last year of a five-year residency, he knew the medical field was not for him. He felt the same way he did thirteen years earlier. The significant difference now — he had a vast amount of expensive school loans.

Understand Conviction
Conviction consists of three elements:

1. Doable Goal
2. Emotional Meaning
3. Mental Drive

How many times have you heard, "You need a goal?" You roll your eyes and mumble, "No shiplap. Tell me something I don't know." Perhaps, you've set your goal, and then day by day, it slowly slips away until your goal never surfaces in your thoughts.

Without emotional investment in the goal, it's a done deal before you <u>ever</u> start. You don't have enough skin in the game. With an emotional driver in place, you can ask the questions that will take you one step at a time to the destination. Think about the athletes you know. Not the athletes who have the body and talent to match the sport, such as Ben Rothlisberger or LeBron James. Although, this isn't about taking anything away from the accomplishments of these great athletes. Instead, let's consider the athletes who have had the odds against them, such as Bethany Hamilton and Chris Paul. (More about these athletes to come.)

Whether in sports, business, or life, people face adversity, overcome it, and Bounce-Up. Let's look at what it takes to have Conviction.

Design a Doable Goal

To start, let's name your goal. What goal do you want to reach? Be careful it isn't a BHAG, also known as "A Big Hairy Audacious Goal." A BHAG can set you up to fail. Instead, let's create a doable goal that sets you up to succeed. You can work toward a BHAG, or better yet, a stretch goal as you start checking achievable goals off your list.

Set yourself up for success by creating a goal that includes:
- Doable. Can reach the goal by yourself or with help. With consistent action, you can achieve it. A goal needs to be clear and specific, not general. My team needs to

increase sales. My team needs to enroll three new clients each by the end of the month. Clear and specific.

- Actionable. Outline the actions you need to get the outcome you want.
- Aimable. Aim for a specific targeted date that you will complete each step. With a deadline date, there's a target you're aiming to hit.

Obtaining a goal relies on the action. The bad habits you break, and the priority actions you make. To help you reach that goal, and to bounce-up, you need the Emotional Meaning behind that goal.

Uncover Emotional Meaning

What is Emotional Meaning? The heartfelt reason you will persist regardless of the obstacles to achieve your goal. Actions create risk. Most people avoid risk. Unfortunately, when you avoid risk, you become immobilized because you're afraid risk will bring pain. Risk can. Uncertainty can bring joy, too. Risk can help you reach your goals.

Here's how Emotional Meaning develops your Bounce-Up Factor.

- Emotional Meaning outweighs a risk you take.
- Emotional Meaning gives you the reason to throw out the excuses to get it done.
- Emotional Meaning provides a genuine reason to achieve a goal.

Emotions carry you through the journey. Emotions drive you to do what you wouldn't consider possible.

Build Mental Drive

What is Mental Drive? The tunnel-vision focus that enables you to ignore the obstacles and propels you forward so that you can reach your destination, your goal.

- The mental focus you need to see the finish line regardless of the naysayers.
- The mental toughness you need to stay on the journey when you want to give up.
- The Mental Drive you need so that you can pursue your goal when everything else is against you.

Mental Drive becomes part of the determining factor because let's face it, it's easy to hit your goal when times are good. It's an entirely different story when times are turbulent, when the disruptions occur, when the tide pushes against you.

Soul Surfer Embodies Conviction

In 2003, thirteen-year-old Bethany Hamilton lost her arm when a 14-foot tiger shark attacked her while surfing in Kauai, Hawaii. Think of the roadblocks that could stop her from getting on a surfboard again. Fear of another shark attack could stop her. Think it would go through your head? It would mine. Bethany could allow victim mentality to keep her from the water and her passion. Then, there's the inner sabotage. Wow. Imagine all the verbal drama that could occur. *Why did this happen to me? What did I do to deserve this? I'll never be able to surf again.*

The drama could bounce inside anyone's head forever. The negative forces were against Bethany Hamilton. No one would've blamed her if she had never jumped on another surfboard again. She ignored the fear that another shark could be in the water. She ignored the Verbal Drama that having one arm would throw her off balance. Bethany climbed on her surfboard within a month of leaving the hospital and Bounced Up to ride her first wave with a single arm. Two years later, Bethany won a championship title, and two years after that title win, at the age of seventeen, she hit the professional surfing circuit. Bethany Hamilton's actions demonstrate Mental Drive.

Power Buzz:
#HotDogPrincess

In 2016, five-year-old Ainsley Turner attended dance class dressed in a hot dog costume. Dance students could wear their favorite costumes during "Princess Week," and everyone, except Ainsley, dressed as a princess. At five, Ainsley's Conviction of what she considered her favorite costume outweighed any thought of following the crowd. When dance teacher Jillian Ackerman tweeted, "In a world full of princesses, be a hot dog," with Ainsley's photo and #HotDogPrincess, it went viral in the Twittersphere.

Behind-the-Scene with Mj:
Go Left When Others Go Right

Traditionally, in an amusement park, most people go right and start at the front of the park. With many Disney tour books pointing this out, park-goers have adjusted their way of thinking. Consider what you want to do that others are doing. Then, watch how they are accomplishing it. Does it make sense to go left when others go right? Can you go against the crowd? When I became single again, my attorney asked if I wanted to go back to my maiden name because that's what most women do if they're changing their name. At least that's what she told me.

I didn't want to take back my maiden name. That person hadn't existed in twenty-some years. She was naïve and young. I couldn't imagine having my maiden name again. Instead, I told her I wanted to change my name legally. My attorney gave me a Santa's naughty list of why I shouldn't do it. Friends' husbands shared why they thought it was a bad idea. Relatives thought I had gone off the deep end.

A common response from friends, "Why? Only celebrities change their names."

"Because I'm not a celebrity, I shouldn't do it?" Determined, I talked to my young adult kids separately so they could understand why I wanted to change my name.

- When I had taken their dad's name, we committed to a lifelong relationship, and that commitment ended.
- It didn't feel right to keep a name that I agreed to take twenty-some years ago without the commitment.
- My kids were through their school years and the name change wouldn't create confusion.

My reason, I wasn't the same person I was when I had taken the name. Let's face it. The more significant reason— I was rebuilding my life and wanted a fresh start. If you missed that story, see Chapter 2.

"Mj Callaway. I LOVE it. It has such an artsy feel to it," my daughter said when I shared, I would legally change my surname and would not go back to my maiden name.

"But all your book are under your married name," my son responded.

"I'll write more books," I assured him, "and they will be under Callaway. I'll use my former married name as a pen name."

With their blessings, I started the name change process without my attorney. After petitioning the court, getting fingerprinted by the State Police to make sure I wasn't a criminal in hiding, paying for two public notices in newspapers about the name change, checking financial standing, paying all the court costs, and appearing in court, the judge granted my petition to legally change my surname to Callaway. Woohoo! I celebrated in a quaint coffee café across the street from the courthouse.

Think About Your Goal

Your goal might not be to change your name, start over, or reinvent yourself. Maybe you only want to change the way you spell your first name like my former co-worker Tom Saxton who changed his spelling to Thom and ordered new business cards. With Tom being a common name, he wanted to stand out from other Toms by spelling it, Thom. He could now say, "Thom with an 'h.'" Or your goal could be a promotion, developing an app, or starting a business. Know, whatever you choose, you can do it when you have Conviction.

Honor Cultivates Conviction

In 2005, during Chris Paul's senior year as a West Forsyth High School basketball player, his grandfather Nathaniel Jones was murdered. Chris dedicated his next basketball game to his grandfather Jones. The high school senior wanted to score 61 points, one point for every year his grandfather was alive. To gain perspective on this incredible feat, Chris averaged 30.8 points during this same season. For most people, and even Chris without the emotional meaning behind it, scoring 61 points would be a BHAG.

Chris's goal had an emotional meaning attached to it and pushed him. At the end of the game, Chris had 61 points. When there is an emotional investment at stake, Conviction occurs. Conviction conquers any roadblocks that hinder you from Bouncing-Up and reaching your goal. Chris's drive led to a successful basketball career with several National Basketball Association (NBA) teams, including the LA Clippers, Houston Rockets, and Oklahoma City Thunder.

Let's break down Chris Paul's Conviction and Bounce-Up Factor.

1. Chris's goal:
    a. Chris's goal was to score 61 points in the game.
2. The emotional meaning behind Chris's goal:
    b. To honor his grandfather
3. The mental drive for Chris
    c. To score one point for each year his grandfather was alive.

Behind the Scene with Mj: Conviction Over Adversity

During the intense Magic Wand (aka chemo treatment), going to Influence, the premier conference for speakers, became my goal. What did I need to do to get to this conference? I needed to stay healthy because of the intense treatment program, which included in this order:

- Six months of Magic Wand;
- One month off to recover before surgery;
- Surgery;
- One month to recover before starting another round of treatment;
- Eight more months of Magic Wand, coinciding with;
- Six weeks of Buzz, aka Radiation, that would end before the conference.

The physicians doubted this would happen because of the intensity of the first round of Magic Wand. One of the medical staff shared I would probably be hospitalized along the treatment journey. Another shared that the seven-hour-long cocktail I received wasn't given to anyone with a compromised immune system because they wouldn't make it. I asked what that meant. Yes, it implied what you think it means. I wouldn't be writing this book.

The first Magic Wand session was two days before Thanksgiving and the beginning of a horrible flu season. To stay healthy, I needed to protect myself from winter illnesses and keep my immune system as stable as possible as the cocktail continued to destroy it. For every situation, both personal and professional, I would ask questions such as, "Will this get me to my goal? Will this hinder my progress? Will this put my health in jeopardy? Is this a good step for me to take?"

During this illness, as a solopreneur, I had to maintain clients, too. Although I was down for the first seven to eight days after Magic Wand, what I called my sofa-surfing period, I used the time for client strategy-creation. I needed to go through treatment as productively, gracefully, and positively as I could. Not one client knew what was happening behind-the-scene.

The same way I protected my physical health I protected my mental health. Only a select group of people and my Power Team knew about the health challenge. I wanted to protect myself from other people's Verbal Drama, the sympathy sorry, and gloom and doom. Having a positive mindset was crucial for me because I work with companies to set their teams up for success by becoming resilient over rejections. I had two goals wrapped into this one adversity.

I skipped holiday parties, networking events, and Sunday church. I was Convicted to my journey, which included staying healthy so I could continue the treatments on time, conserve my energy for clients meetings, and hit my goal. By eliminating situations with crowds, I had a better chance of staying healthy. The Conviction Goal was twofold: to be a role model for my kids and clients and to attend Influence. On July 5, 2017, I finished the last Buzz session, and on July 6, 2017, I boarded the plane to Orlando, Florida, to attend my first Influence Conference.

Let's define each goal.
1. Mj's goal:
   a. Be positive and gracious during the tough road of treatment ahead.
2. Mj's emotional meaning behind the goal:
   b. Being the only available parent, I needed to be a positive role model for my kids because every day we face setbacks.
   c. To go through the year-long treatment program without my clients knowing the doctor's diagnosis.

3. Mj's mental drive to reach this goal:

   d. I couldn't give mouth service to this goal. I had to set an example in action that it's about how we Bounce-Up from the setback.

   e. Providing a positive example for my kids and clients drove my actions.

   f. How could I possibly say, "You can do it," when adversity strikes my family or clients unless I lead by example.

Game Changers:
Up-level Your Game

1. Track it. "What gets measured, gets done," is an often-said statement in business. Apply that motto to your goal, career, life, or whatever it is you want to shift. In Chris Paul's example, the scoreboard tracked his progress. Track your progress with the innovative site StickK.com. I used this site to track my weekly commitment to finishing this book. I had eight weeks to hit my targeted deadline. I joined StickK, committed to daily writing, selected my like-minded communities, assigned my referee, and my consequence if I didn't succeed. Each week I reported my progress to my communities.

2. Start a challenge. Challenges are prevalent on social media platforms to pull in new followers. Challenges motivate. When I started working out again, my son challenged me to hit the gym for 18 straight days. "You'll want to keep going," he said. His challenge motivated me because I wanted to prove I could do it. To be accountable, I posted daily with #day17ofchallengedone on social media.

3. Focus with intensity. Ignore what you can't change. Focus with an Ironman intensity on what you can do and what you can control.

4. Establish an on/off system. Work for a designated time block, then take a mini-break. For example, work for 30 minutes. Take five minutes off. This system reminds me of the ice on, ice off method when you injure an ankle. (Psst. Remove all distractions during your time block.) Increase your time block gradually. For those starting, begin with 15 minutes on and 5 minutes off. Think of each time block as a ten-yard pass going down the field, getting closer to the goal line.

5. Protect yourself. As you're growing and gaining momentum, you could run into people that want you to stay in the same place. Recognize the people who are not suitable for your mission. Limit time with them if you need to do so, or cut the cord altogether. I know this isn't easy to do because I had to do it when I was going through treatment. In the end, your future self will thank you. Stay strong. Surround yourself with people who have similar goals, ambitions, and aspirations as you do. People on your team, your Power Team.

6. Image your future self. As your future self, how would you act? Where do you want to be in your career, business, and life? Who do you want to have in your life? When will you have achieved this vision? Describe your future world to yourself in a letter at FutureMe.org.

Bounce-Up
Momentum

- Conviction occurs when you have a goal, an emotional meaning attached to the target, and mental drive focus to reach the goal.
- To achieve goal success, create a doable goal and a stretch goal.
- Tie emotions to your goal because emotions drive actions.
- Mental Drive is a tunnel-vision focus, mental toughness to block out or eliminate the obstacles and naysayers, and the drive to pursue your goal with conviction.

Boost Your Bounce-Up Factor:
Strengthen Conviction

Develop your Conviction to increase your Bounce-Up Factor. Now, it's your turn.

1. What emotional meaning will push you to reach your goal?
2. What will drive you to achieve it?
3. Who can help keep you accountable?
4. What is one takeaway you gained from this chapter?
5. What is one positive action you will take?

Wordology
BHAG: "A Big Hairy Audacious Goal."

Conviction: Confidence and a strong belief that you can achieve a goal.

Emotional Meaning: A genuine and heartfelt reason you want to achieve a goal.

Mental Drive: The tunnel-vision focus that enables you to ignore the obstacles to reach your goal.

Stretch Goal: An ambitious goal you set that deliberately challenges.

Part III

People Who Bounced-Up™

CHAPTER 8
On the Healthy Side of Life: Despair Can't Keep Me Down

"A closed door signals it's time for action in a new direction." - **Mjism**

"How did I get here?" Chef Wes Stepp asked himself. He felt lost. Thinking back, he thought, *Why did I go left when I could've gone right?*

You might have asked similar questions. Wondering how life would've turned out had you taken a different path.

A well-known chef and restaurant owner in a small town in the Outer Banks of North Carolina, as the tourist season of 2014 wound down, Wes found himself in the middle of a high-profile divorce. Add the unfortunate timing to the mix—it was the worst financial season, fall heading into winter for a chef-owner in a tourist town. The annual Outer Banks Taste of the Beach Festival held in March, propelling restaurant bookings and catering events, was six months away. Wes's remorse about past decisions came into play, filling his brain with all the Verbal Drama that worked against him.

"We look ten years in the past, or we look two years in the future," Wes said, "and either way, fear sets in." Fear stormed in for Wes. Fear of vanishing finances with winter approaching. Doubt about what the future might or might not bring. Fear he would be stuck in that hole of despair and not get out.

Can't Stop Growth

"When you feel lost, you don't know which way to go," Wes admitted. "Do you stay where you are? Or do you go in the other direction? What do you do?"

During a conversation, a friend says matter-of-factly, "It's okay. You're going through an A.F.G.E."

"What is it?"

"Another f**king growth experience," his friend answered. "You found yourself in a growth change."

"I don't want to grow," Wes said, adamantly.

"You don't have a choice," the friend responded. "Wes, we have to grow."

"If you're going through an A.F.G.E., you think it's a serious problem," Wes admitted. "Yet, when someone else says you're going through it, you can tell they don't see it the way you do. It isn't presenting as such a big deal for them. They're not feeling the emotions, the desperation, and the dark hole. But you're convinced you will be in this place for the rest of your life."

Lost Once Before

This setback wasn't the first time Wes found himself lost. Twenty years ago, Wes turned to sobriety. Through the 12-Step Program and his spirituality, Wes celebrated his 20th anniversary days before his interview for this book. Wes thought life would be better in sobriety. But the Outer Banks chef lost more in sobriety than he lost when he was drinking. Wes couldn't fathom it. He married and divorced in sobriety. He started businesses and lost businesses in sobriety.

When Wes turned to sobriety, he also turned to physical fitness. He hit the gym. Working out was his escape from feeling lost, from all the emotional drama in his head. And working out allowed him to consume the pizza, burgers, and soda he enjoyed.

Hard Times Pile High

With the high-profile divorce, vanishing reservations, and feelings of despair, working out kept Wes in the present, until he injured his knee during this emotional period. After surgery repaired a meniscus tear, he tried going back to his old workout routine and couldn't. He didn't have an escape from the Verbal Drama in his head. Stir in his consumption of unhealthy food along with his lack of exercise, and it all took a toll on him physically and mentally.

Weeks slipped into months before Wes hobbled into the gym for his first workout post-surgery. "I realized I couldn't work out the same way I always did." His troubles continued to boil like hot water until a gym friend suggested Wes start a new goal and enter a bodybuilding competition.

Develop a Recipe with a Goal

"I've never been a bodybuilder," Wes told his friend. "I'm a chef. I can't eat like you. Boiled chicken, oatmeal, brown rice, and sweet potatoes," Wes recited, "gray food. I love food more than I love fitness. I'm a chef."

The gym friend told Wes to create food he would eat within the parameters of the required food regimen he would need to eat as fuel for the competition. Wes discovered he had to reinvent how he cooked. He had to taper the oils, fats, and empty-calorie ingredients that he regularly used.

"I had to have good flavor without useless calories," Wes shared his eye-opening discovery. "When I concentrated on healthy food, the food would bring me back to the present, so I didn't go back into that dark hole of pain."

Meals become food for the body and soul. The bodybuilding competition gave the chef a set three-step goal:

- A three-month deadline;
- A workout regiment, and;
- A food recipe.

Another lesson Wes learned: he realized he needed to eat every three hours regardless of whether he felt hungry or not. It had taken Wes some time to wrap his head around that requirement—the importance of food fueling the body.

"Wes, it doesn't matter how you feel," his bodybuilding friend, aka his Power Team, said, "**It matters what you do.** It's part of the recipe."

With his goal set, Wes stayed focused on the present instead of the past. He'd have to concentrate on healthy, flavorful food, which pushed him to stay present. At the end of three months, the forty-something-year-old chef stood on a stage in front of 250 people. He was ripped.

"I felt like I could climb Mt. Everest."

The experience led Wes to a new opportunity, as a partner in Tastefully Fit, a healthy meal-plan system. As chef-owner of Red Sky Café, his restaurant serves healthy fare and provides meal alternatives to guests who have food allergies or specific diets.

Wes's Bounce-Up
Momentum

- Wes applied his knowledge about ingredients to help him develop healthy, tasty food that would enable him to achieve his goal. Utilizing his experience and food know-how supported his belief that he could do it.
- He realized he needed to stay present. He kept his head out of the past and future to concentrate on the present moment.
- He moved mentally. Wes didn't stay in the same place with "can't do" and "victim mentality." He completed one step at a time to reach his goal.
- Wes recognized these actions were only a small part in reaching his goal. In addition to reaching out to his gym friend, Wes relied on his spirituality because it had served him well when he turned to sobriety.

Wes's Bounce-Up
Power

Wes understands tasty food is essential to him. After all, he is a chef and loves food more than fitness. By developing recipes that he could enjoy while fueling his body for the upcoming competition, he stays true to his self and brand. Wes recognized how his dark time transformed his way of life and spilled into positive growth for his business.

Wes's Game Changers:
Move Forward

1. Get out of yourself. Self takes you to the darkness. Get out of yourself by choosing a goal more compelling than you are. It's there on the shelf. Pull it off. Don't think that you're too old to achieve it. You can do it. Give your goal a deadline.

2. Create a system to reach your goal. Wes's bodybuilding friend weighed Wes in every Monday. They worked out five days a week. Wes ate every three hours according to the eating plan his friend recommended. Wes had a system to be in the best place for the competition.

3. Make a move. If you find yourself in an unfavorable place in your life, make some moves. Change where you live. Change the furniture, décor, or paint color. Or move to a new location. You don't have to move states away. You don't have to make major changes. You only need to make a move. Take one step at a time. Get up. Get yourself out. It doesn't matter how you feel. It matters what you do.

Boost Your Bounce-Up Factor:
A Goal Bigger Than You

1. What is a goal that is bigger than you are?
2. What system can you implement to reach your goal?
3. Who has prior experience related to your goal?
4. What is one takeaway you gained from this chapter?
5. What is one positive action you will take?

CHAPTER 9
Initiate a New Identity: Don't Stay Lost in the Past

"You can't control life's faceplants. You can control how you Bounce Up." **- Mjism**

Pam Kinzler found herself juggling many balls in her prominent position as a high school principal of more than 1,400 students. She was on track to be the next school district superintendent. She juggled the commitments and responsibility of being a high school principal and running a household of four, including a teenage son who was smoking marijuana and heading down the wrong path.

"In hindsight, my son was one of those kids I talked about as a principal, and I didn't know it," Pam said.

This power woman was keeping everything afloat, until doctors diagnosed her with dystonia, a disease called the twisting disease. Dystonia causes parts of a person's body to twist involuntarily due to a muscle disorder, in which the muscles contract uncontrollably. Dystonia added one more ball to juggle. Within six months of the onset of dystonia, Pam started to drop the balls. To alleviate some of the pressure at work, Pam moved into a teaching position in the same school.

"This was the beginning of the end of my career," Pam admitted.

Moving into a teaching position didn't work for numerous reasons. The school staff continued to treat Pam like the principal. She never really fit in as a teacher, and dystonia didn't get better. The more her brain tried to work, the less her brain could control the twisting of her body.

Stop the Juggling Act

"I felt like life was a juggling act, and something had to go. I had to give up one of those balls. I couldn't give up my family. I couldn't give up my home. Though I wanted to give up dystonia, I was stuck with it," Pam shared. "The only ball I could give up was my job."

She gave up the career she loved, the future she planned, and lost her identity in the process.

Closet Reveals Identity

Controlling dystonia with medications took two years. Two years during which she couldn't figure out who she was now. "Who was the real Pam? I had a closetful of suits, dresses, shoes, and handbags. I identified with my work clothing. This closet was my identity and who I was…"

Pam's closet held only one pair of jeans, which made her feel a wretched awareness of how much she associated with her wardrobe, because her position consumed her. Crying, Pam emptied her closet. Her entire wardrobe went from the closet onto her bed. She kept two suits: one for weddings and one for funerals. She kept one handbag and two pairs of dress shoes.

She called the local women's shelter and asked if they wanted her career attire. The next day, the tears continued as she and her husband loaded her car with what was now her past.

"I felt good, the clothing would help someone else." Afterward, Pam went shopping. "That was fun. I never had many casual clothes. I bought workout outfits and sneakers because they were more comfortable for me."

Find Humor during Setbacks

After dystonia hit, Pam and her husband Greg chose to skip the family's Sunday Pittsburgh Steelers parties. Although they were dedicated fans, the medication made it difficult to participate. During one game, the couple snuggled on their oversized chair. Trying out a new drug, Pam fell asleep during Super Bowl XLIII, the Steelers vs. Cardinals game where Santonio Holmes created a famous play when his toes stayed inside the boundary line for the touchdown while his body flew out-of-bounds. Not wanting to wake her, Greg couldn't yell, cheer, or root for Holmes's crucial play, which won the game.

During Pam's next medical appointment, she told the doctor she needed to go off that drug because it made her fall asleep and missed the touchdown. Her physician said to the resident doctor, "See where your patient's priorities are when you work in Pittsburgh?"

Pam laughed at the puzzled expression on the resident doctor's face.

Disability Meets Ability and Opportunity

"All your leadership training is a myth," Pam said. "Reality is you never know where the Y in the road will come, and you need to be ready to bounce rather than take those step-by-step actions taught in many leadership classes. Instead, be that ball and go with it and stay positive."

Pam used the time she now had as an opportunity to get her son back on track, making momentous decisions from changing schools to strict boundaries with friends and activities.

Now, Pam viewed dystonia as a gift instead of a disability. To her, the word disability meant a link between ability and opportunity. Had she still been working, she wouldn't have had the time and connection with her son. Her son's path might be different today. He could've been another teen statistic instead of graduating from Penn State with a Bachelor in Engineering as an Academic All-American in water polo.

Pam's Bounce-Up
Momentum

- Pam realized that her colleagues could not move past seeing her as the principal. Her colleagues would keep her stuck in that leadership role.
- She recognized her health and family were more important to her than the career she loved.
- Pam used her principal wisdom to set her son on the right path for his future.

Pam's Bounce-Up
Power

Pam looked at her life and considered what balls she could juggle and what had to go. She infused her closet with clothes that would fit her new lifestyle while giving her career wardrobe to others who could use it. She changed her perspective and found ways to see the humorous side of a situation. When the timing was right, Pam returned to contributing to her community by helping plan and participant in her town's first National Night Out event

---

Pam's Game Changers: Create Your Identify

1. Look deeper than the surface. Take time to find out what's real in life versus what you think to be authentic. "There were a lot of people who wanted to be friends with me because of the position I held. I learned the hard way that I had few friends—less than five."
2. Create your mantra. Pam's mantra: *Be content with what you have, rejoice in the way things are.* When you realize nothing is lacking, the world belongs to you.
3. Give back to the community. Pam was a big part of her school district, which was a different district than where she lived. She was well-known and lost that piece of belonging when she left her position. Once she had her life balanced, she joined a non-profit in her home community. The first event she helped to plan was First National Night Out.

Boost Bounce-Up Factor: Reinvent What Isn't Working

1. What would be your mantra? Create your mantra and place it where you can see it regularly.
2. Have you worked through your emotions? Experience them and move on.

3. Were you once a part of a community, group, or organization that you've avoided? Is it time to connect again or start a new interest?
4. What is one takeaway you gained from this chapter?
5. What is one positive action you will take?

CHAPTER 10
Your Journey Isn't What You Expected: So, Now What!

"One question can change your life." - **Mjism**

In 2010, corporate marketing specialist Summer Owens faced another one of life's setbacks as she found herself recently divorced, 31 years old, and building a new life with her teenage son. Although it wouldn't be as life-altering as being a teen mom with a newborn, Summer knew she managed adversity best when she had a purpose and a plan. Those two ingredients had guided her when she found herself pregnant after a forced sexual encounter on her 15th birthday. As she shifted into a new routine as a single mom again, Summer knew what her next plan would be and the purpose for it.

"Colleagues and friends would ask me, 'How did you do it?' While I was in high school, I had worked two part-time jobs to support my son and me. People wanted to know how I managed being a teen mom; finishing high school, college, and graduate school at the top of my class; and work," shared Summer.

"I didn't have time to think about how I did it; **I just did it**." The words rushed out as if Summer re-experienced her frantic days.

"I prioritized my future ambitions over my present fun. My grades and my son were my focus. Every minute of every day had a purpose," Summer continued. "The hour between getting out of high school and going to work was dedicated to taking care of my son and starting my homework."

Beat the Odds

"How did you do it?" became the impetus Summer needed to sit down and write *Life After Birth: A Memoir of Survival and Success as a Teenage Mother.* "I wrote the book to show teen moms that they didn't have to drop out of school. I earned my MBA, worked full-time, and raised my son. I wanted other teen moms to know they could continue their education and go to college."

Summer knew the statistics. Only 53 percent of teen mothers complete a traditional high school degree, and another 17 percent earn a high school equivalency diploma through GED testing. Compare it to the 90 percent of women who were not teen moms who receive a traditional high school diploma. Only 2 percent of teen moms earn their college degree by the time they hit 30 years old.

Teen Mom Turned Author

A soon-to-be published author, she cried as she put her story to paper. "Some were good tears because I knew what hurt me, but some tears surprised me because I suppressed my emotions."

In her book, the marketing executive shared how she turned the emotional struggles and hardships into a positive perspective. "I focused on the fact that I was a teen mother, which pushed me to think beyond myself. It matured me faster and motivated me to be successful, not just for myself, but for my son."

With a published book in hand, she never expected the variety of ages in her readership. She never expected the therapeutic endeavor to kick off a string of new opportunities. "People read it," Summer shared, enthusiastically, as if it still surprises her today. "People were inspired. The comments I would hear, 'Reading your story showed me that I can make it, too.'"

In addition to the teen mom readers, which she expected, women and men in their 30s, 40s, and older read *Life After Birth*.

"Helping others and sharing my advice gave me this new energy. I felt like I had found my purpose. I used my marketing background [with Memphis Grizzlies, ServiceMaster and FedEx] to promote my book which led to requests to speak—especially at schools. Although I'm shy and don't like to focus on me, I took the speaking opportunities because I wanted to sell more books and get my message out."

Her marketing plan worked. Radio, television, newspapers, and magazines featured Summer and her inspiring advice.

Opportunities Surface Unexpectedly

With the publicity of her book, paid opportunities emerged, such as speaking at schools and organizations. Getting paid speaking engagements grew organically for Summer and turned into what entrepreneurial gurus consider a side hustle, while she continued working as a marketing executive.

"One night, I said my prayers and asked for a business name that embodied my message, and 'S.O. What!' came to me." Excitement weaved into Summer's voice. "Oprah has her name in her companies and I thought because my business is so much about my life that I could incorporate my name subtly."

Although S.O. in S.O. What! stands for Summer Owens, the bigger meaning behind the business name is based on the Serenity Prayer. Saying, "So what!" means accepting the things in your life that you can't change. The "So NOW What?" in her logo means taking steps to change what can be changed.

"Saying 'so what!' takes the power away from your problems, eliminates excuses, overcomes obstacles and focuses on solutions," said Summer.

With the surge of publicity and an increase in speaking fees, operating her business full-time became a viable option. In 2013, Summer created a three-to-five-year exit plan, until her company offered a buyout. With the minimum requirement met, at the age of 33, she applied. Unfortunately, Summer got denied the buyout that would give her a financial cushion as she pursued entrepreneurship.

Leaving a job you love with a steady paycheck takes guts and faith. With some savings and the belief that with more available time her side hustle would grow, Summer left her 15-year marketing career with financial security behind.

"Speaking engagements didn't come as regularly after I left my corporate position as they did when I was working full-time or at least it didn't seem like it."

Entrepreneurship Isn't Easy

The author-turned-business woman depleted her savings and dipped into the IRA she started at age 23 because she believed it was crucial to save for the future. Like many entrepreneurs, she racked up credit card debt, too, which went against Summer's steadfast belief to spend wisely — the one main principle that enabled her to provide for herself and her son as a struggling teen mom.

"I'm uncomfortable with debt. Whenever I bought a new vehicle, I paid it off in six months or less."

At this time, credit cards financed her business and her life. She was in the proverbial catch-22 dilemma. She didn't have the funds to invest in her business, yet she couldn't afford not to do so. She bought books on credit cards. She paid for conferences and memberships, such as the National Speakers Association (NSA), on credit cards.

"Often, I contemplated going back to my corporate position with that comfortable paycheck," admitted Summer, "because I didn't get the buyout, I could return to the company. I'd contemplate going back; then, I would get a call or email from someone saying how much I had helped them or even saved them. It was deep." She paused as emotion took over.

"People shared they wanted to drop out of school, some were pregnant, or they thought about suicide. I'd look at those reminders…those reminders, my faith, and my belief in myself told me to stick with it."

One Question Can Change Your Life

With the ongoing request for advice, Summer added a coaching component to her speaking and book business.

Although the new service provided some additional revenue, it wasn't enough to be self-sustaining. She needed something bigger.

"Have you considered aligning your curriculum to the state standards? It would be perfect for that since students love reading your book," a local guidance counselor who had used Summer's original curriculum asked.

Summer thought *I can do this work. I can see the path.* Summer now had a definitive plan to correspond with her purpose, the two ingredients that worked for her as a teen mom. She jumped on the idea, revising her original curriculum to align to academic standards and teach literacy, life skills, and character education.

Over the next few years, several local schools invested in Summer's curriculum and workbooks. Five years into her business, it wasn't precisely where Summer wanted to be financially. With her bigger vision at the forefront, this driven entrepreneur continued to pitch her data-proven course to educational leaders.

In June of 2018, after working her marketing plan and sharing her purpose, her vision came to life and her financial picture finally changed. Summer was awarded a contract to implement her program in one of the largest school districts in the United States.

"This contract solidified my work," she said humbly. "My story is now my career. I get to use my challenges and my victories, my life, to educate, encourage, and inspire others."

Summer's Bounce-Up Momentum

- Summer wrote her book because people consistently asked her for advice. There's an adage *Our customers tell us what business we're in.* Clearly, Summer was in the "Ask Summer" advice business.
- Summer pulled from her personal and professional experiences to start and grow her business.
- Summer created and revised her curriculum to align with state academic standards, which filled a void.

Summer's Bounce-Up Power

She turned adversity into an opportunity. Summer used her experience in a positive way so that others could rise above their current situations.

Summer's Game Changers: So Now What?

1. Recognize what makes you happy. When Summer's coaching clients inquire, "How do you find your purpose?" Summer asks:
   a. What makes you happy?
   b. What are you doing when you feel fulfilled?
   c. If money wasn't a factor, what would you do every day?
2. Know what hurts. On the opposite end of happy, Summer suggests you think about what hurts? Understanding

what hurts can be useful, too, in finding what you were meant to do.

3. Hear the needs expressed. Discover the void or gap exposed. Then, find a solution or way to fill the void.

Boost Your Bounce-Up Factor:
What Need Can You Solve?

1. What question are you not asking yourself?
2. What need has someone expressed that you can solve?
3. How can your know-how fill a void that has been exposed?
4. What is one takeaway you gained from this chapter?
5. What is one positive action you will take?

CHAPTER 11
Your Past Doesn't Define You: Start Your Own Movement

"Each day you have the choice to create a new story you love." - **Mjism**

Sometimes we get stuck in what seems like a vortex of habits. We can't break out of the harmful pattern we're in at that time.

At 28 years old, Sarah Souri celebrated the happiest day in life—her wedding. It was 1994, before cell phones were part of daily life and the beginning of the technology era. The bride and her groom traveled to Niagara Falls for their first trip together as husband and wife. During their honeymoon, using a hotel telephone, Sarah periodically checked in with her mom. During the last phone call, the mother-of-the-bride asked, "When you get back from your honeymoon, will you come home to Ohio to see me?"

What the young bride didn't know: she would be coming home to her mom's funeral. Her mom had just turned 50 years old.

Sarah's mom, Monica Souri, suffered from an autoimmune disease for most of her daughter's childhood. Her mom's illness kept the family close. As the only Indian in her class, Sarah felt she didn't fit in. This situation made her relationship with her mom and family that much stronger.

At Monica's funeral service, the pastor asked if anyone wanted to speak. Sarah stood and shared a funny story about her mom eating mangoes, and everyone laughed, enjoying the memory of mother and daughter, despite the sadness.

Stuck In a Motherless Daughter Moment

As a young newlywed, Sarah moved to a different city, started a new job as a psychotherapist, and lost her mom all at the same time. "My life crashed just days after what was the happiest day of my life—my wedding. I felt lost after mom died."

"A few months after mom passed, I was in a bookstore and came across a book titled *Motherless Daughters* by Hope Edelman," shared Sarah. "I remember looking at the book and thinking '*This book defines me. It defines everything I feel but didn't know how to define it.*'" Sarah paused as if she's standing in that very bookstore, reliving that moment and connecting to other motherless daughters. "Someone else got it. I could put a name to what I was feeling."

During the 20 years she raised kids and continued her career as a psychotherapist, she identified herself as a motherless daughter. In 2014, Sarah launched her private practice, working with motherless daughters.

"While I was growing my practice, I often shared my pitch [usually 60 seconds of information about you or your business] at a networking event. One time I ended my pitch with 'I'm a motherless daughter.'" She paused. "I got a collective 'aww'," she shared with a raw voice.

That collective "aww" created the opening Sarah needed to start shifting what defined her. Sarah realized that characterizing herself solely as a motherless daughter caused her life to plateau. The push she needed came next.

Recognize a Pivotal Moment

"Right before I turned 50, I thought about my mom and all the moments she never experienced. I didn't even know what she wanted to do. I was turning 50, and mom died at 50. This revelation was a pivotal moment. I realized being a motherless daughter was only part of my story. I didn't want people to feel sorry for me," stressed Sarah. "I'm changing my story. I'm living for her and me. What could I do now and still honor my mom?"

Could honoring her mom somehow have stopped Sarah from having fun because her mom wouldn't be able to do so? Could guilt unknowingly have played into Sarah's actions and thoughts?

"Maybe guilt did," Sarah admitted. "Why did I get to live, and she didn't? Why did I get to be healthy and she wasn't. Motherless daughter thoughts stopped me from growing emotionally. Part of you is gone, and you'll never be the same."

Sarah reflected on her mom's funeral service and the mangoes story. She decided to create experiences that she would enjoy for herself and her mom. She could honor her mom in other ways by stepping out of her comfort zone.

"I suddenly realized she would want me to live a full life," Sarah said with a smile.

Transition From Sideline Watching to Dancing Queen

The shift started. Sarah's new mission was to challenge herself by doing activities that scared her. She changed her actions and her presence. Gone were the small, delicate accessories she favored in the past. She swapped them for bold, eye-catching accent pieces she added to her wardrobe. Her newfound love of jewelry gave her style and confidence. More importantly, she felt as if she connected to her mom because her mother loved jewelry, too.

When Sarah's 50th birthday rolled around, she didn't celebrate with the typical "Over the Hill" theme party. Instead, she went back to the 70s.

"My family, friends, and I celebrated by hearing a Pittsburgh-based disco band, Dancing Queen. It was so much fun. After my party, I started following the band," said this once-shy introvert turned band groupie. "I bought bell-bottoms, platform shoes, and a wig to wear. I'd invite friends to join me. The band knows me, and I've been on stage with them, too."

The 1980s movie *Dirty Dancing* comes to mind with Patrick Swayze's famous quote, "Nobody puts Baby in the corner." Sarah stopped watching life from the sidelines and let herself boogie into a new life.

Start Your Own Movement

Sarah's 50th dance party started her own movement. She recalled making everyone laugh at her mom's funeral service, which revived her interest in public speaking. Sarah joined Toastmasters. She had dabbled in Toastmasters once after her first baby, but this time the psychotherapist promised herself she'd make it stick. Coming full circle, her first Toastmasters speech was about Sarah and her mom.

From Toastmasters, this woman on a clear mission registered for an improv class, which led to the National Speakers Association, stand-up comedy, taking voice lessons, singing karaoke, and taking an adult acting class.

Each of these activities gave Sarah confidence and improved her professional skills, which led to being a guest promoting her business on local television shows and podcasts.

What broke the pattern and made the shift for Sarah? "I knew I needed a new normal."

Sarah's Bounce-Up Momentum

- Sarah didn't want her motherless daughter story to be her *only* story.
- She embraced the new activities that would force her to step out of her comfort zone, both in appearance and actions.
- When Sarah stopped focusing specifically on her role as motherless daughter, she grew personally and professionally.

Sarah's Bounce-Up Power

Sarah recognized having her mom pass was what happened to her. It didn't define her. She pulled in what she loved to do to create a fresh story with exciting new experiences that enriched her life.

Sarah's Game Changers: Shift to a New Normal

1. Remember your childhood excitement. What did you love to do? Think back to your childhood. What were you passionate about as a child? Sarah remembered a piano recital and how excited she was to perform, which prompted her love for the stage.
2. Try new opportunities. Be open to something new. Sarah's piano recital memory prompted her to try something new.

She joined Toastmasters, which led her to explore other performance-related activities like improv and stand-up comedy.

3. Surround yourself with new people. When you're stuck in a pattern with the same people, you're likely to stay on the same path. You do the same things. Find new, positive friends to support your unique opportunities and help you grow.

Boost Your Bounce-Up Factor:
Create Your New Normal

1. What situation from your past have you let negatively define you?
2. How has the situation impacted your personal life, career, or business?
3. How can you create a new normal?
4. What is one takeaway you gained from this chapter?
5. What is one positive action you will take?

CHAPTER 12
Fundamental Strength: Who You Are Is Stronger than What You Do

"No one can take away your inner strength." - **Mjism**

In 2011, an ongoing NCAA investigation involving six Ohio State Buckeye players had cast a shadow over Jim Tressel's outstanding performance as the head football coach. While speculation swirled, the investigation revealed Coach Tressel failed to notify Ohio State University (OSU) officials when he learned his players received improper benefits from a local tattoo parlor.

Although the football coach got a hefty fine along with a two-game suspension, he did what was best for his team and OSU and went further. He resigned. How does one Bounce-Up under the unrelenting media coverage when you're a significant part of an active community such as Buckeye Nation?

The former coach viewed this situation as an opportunity for a new direction, though he didn't know what, yet. "I decided that I had done the coaching gig for 37 years or so and always knew I wanted to experience something else at some point," Tressel shared. "You never know when it's going to be. And when the moment came and the pivot needed to be made, it wasn't clear in my mind what direction I wanted to go."

An avid reader, Tressel made a goal. "I wanted to read 100 books about different subjects and not one book would be about football." He used his reading goal as a vehicle to discover where his new path would lead.

A Book Goal Takes a Detour

"I read 32 of the 100 books on my list before Coach Jim Caldwell's request interrupted my reading goal." That interruption was a one-year detour to the Indianapolis Colts.

When Tressel's contract as game-day consultant ended, he now knew his next direction would be in higher education. He could help more students and make a bigger impact.

"After being approached by several headhunters for various positions in education, one door opening lead to another and I found my place at The University of Akron, and eventually to Youngstown State University (YSU)."

Tressel did more than find his place. He became President of YSU. Some people in the academic world would consider this a tremendous feat as most often university presidents have a PhD, whereas the former coach has a BA from Baldwin Wallace University and an MA from University of Akron.

Revive a Game Plan Tradition

In his role in higher education, Tressel used the power of books as part of his game plan to tackle the challenges of higher education. In 2018, the entire YSU Campus read *Winnebagos on Wednesdays: How Visionary Leadership Can Transform Higher Education*. In the summer of 2019, the YSU Deans read John Maxwell's *Leadershift: The 11 Essential Changes Every Leader Must Embrace*.

"I believe you are what you read," says the university president, as he continues to use books as a vehicle for his own self-improvement and to inspire educators, employees, and staff at YSU.

A Few of Tressel's Favorite Books from His 100-Books List

1. *Golf's Sacred Journey* by David L. Cook
2. *Have a Little Faith* by Mitch Albom
3. *Lessons Learned* by William G. Bowen

Adversity Becomes an Indicator

Although Tressel's resignation, reading list, and self-imposed hiatus propelled his pivot into education, his strong fundamentals played an influential part in overcoming adversity.

"The one thing we talked to our student athletes about is you have to have dreams, goals, a great plan, and work hard. There's going to be adversity in your career, game, season, and over your lifetime," says the former Buckeyes coach. "How you handle adversity is going be an indicator of what you're all about. Adversity is inevitable. It's not **if,** it's **when,**" Tressel stressed. "How do you handle it? You need to have your fundamentals. Guidelines you will always go back to regardless of the changes to your game plan."

Life's Fundamentals Build Strong Foundations

One of the university president's fundamental principles is having the awareness to know the difference between **who you are** and **what you do**.

"As a student-athlete," he would tell his student players, "you play football, go to school, get good grades, and lift weights. That's what you do. Who you are is different than what you do."

"Who you are is really what life is all about. Who you are spiritually, morally, and ethically," Tressel continued. "We talked about being grateful. How fortunate we are to have these opportunities. Are you grateful for opportunities on and off the field?"

He emphasized building strong relationships with family and friends and how important it is to value relationships. "Having goals in relationships is part of developing who you are. Developing who you are is as important to us [coaches] as what you do on the field. Who you are is constantly being developed and evolves into what you do."

Fundamentals Outpower Setbacks

Tressel and Youngstown, Ohio share a common theme—both have endured adversity. With the shutdown of the Campbell Works Mill in 1977 and General Motors Lordstown plant in 2019, Youngstown faced setbacks. Both, Tressel and Youngstown, have bounced-up.

"All of our human journeys and most of our locations [cities], have a time when things are going one way or another. Some call it ups and downs. Although the 'downs' propel you more than the 'ups.'"

Bouncing-Up can be difficult in any circumstances. Bouncing-Up in the public eye and with the media trailing your every move is a considerable challenge. Two key ingredients provide the University President the base he needs to overcome setbacks.

1. Curiosity. President Tressel has always been inquisitive, which spurs him to ask, "How can we get this done?" (See Chapter 6 for additional questions to increase your curiosity and ability to improvise.)

2. Gratitude. Being grateful for his opportunities, and people who invested in him has always been a part of the former football coach's fundamentals. Recognize you can't do it alone. Thank the people who invested in you and supported you.

See Possibilities

It is more than likely you know some people who see opportunities, and some who don't. What creates that insight to see a positive when it could look like a negative?

"It's a mindset and an attitude. If you're looking for opportunities, you'll find team. If you don't think there are any opportunities, you won't find them."

There's a quintessential difference between those who Bounce-Up and those who don't. Those who don't let the roadblocks stop them and they blamed others. One belief that has guided the university president—he assigns the responsibility to himself to use and move forward from the experiences he's had.

"I realize I've been so fortunate to have had the parents I've had, the teachers, coaches, mentors, and experiences. I'm of the mindset that shame on me if I can't overcome adversity because I've had a great deal of modeling, training, and experiencing."

President Tressel's Bounce-Up Momentum

- Before the former coach made a pivot, he paused. He used the time off as an opportunity to determine what his next decision would be.
- Creating the book list goal and accepting the consulting position enabled him to evaluate his next direction.
- President Tressel's fundamentals, which included curiosity, gratitude, and a positive mindset, helped him to see opportunities.

President Tressel's Bounce-Up Power

Jim uses books as a resource for every phase of life. He knows how to take a step back, pivot, and see opportunities. He has a game plan to assess, evaluate, and focus on the next direction.

President Tressel's Game Changer: Activate a Game Plan

The former football coach had a rule of three for his team. "Because players had play after play, they didn't have time to say, 'Oh, aren't I wonderful because it worked?' or 'Woe is me' when it didn't." The same rule of three that worked for the Buckeyes football team can work for you at any moment in your life.

- Assess. Quickly access what it is you did. How could you have done it better? What did you learn from it? You can't let the last play affect the next play. You need the same mindset at any moment in life. You can't allow your past to impact your next decision.

- Evaluate. Look at the situation. "In football, maybe it's 2nd and three," says the former coach. "Here's the ball placement. What is the condition? Where are we at this moment?" Whether you are going through a situation from which you need to Bounce-Up from or going through a situation where you need to stay up, evaluation is key to success.

- Focus. Focus on the call, situation, or your reality. Tressel uses a football situation as an example. "In football, what is the play being sent in? What is being asked of you? What is your responsibility for the next play?" In life, what is the next opportunity or reality? "In my case, my situation was different because I didn't have to storm back to work to put food on the table," says Tressel said. "I wanted to read 100 books. I was older, further along in my career, and our four children were grown and gone." Have your mindset right for the next play to be successful. In facing adversity or success, it's the same mindset. See what the next opportunity will be. Get your mind right based on what you need to be successful.

Boost Your Bounce-Up Factor:
Write Your Playbook

1. How has a past challenge propelled you forward?
2. What current situation or goal do you need to evaluate?
3. Where do you need to focus so you can get to your goal line?
4. What is one takeaway you gained from this chapter?
5. What is one positive action you will take?

CHAPTER 13
A Silver Lining: Devastation Can't Stop a Community

"Let your Power Team be your foundation when standing alone isn't an option." – **Mjism**

"The fire was not determined to be arson, though it was suspected," shared Vicki Basnight co-owner of Basnight's Lone Cedar Restaurant.

On May 1, 2007, Vicki left the restaurant after midnight, eager to go home and get some sleep. In less than 20 minutes from the time she locked the restaurant's doors, her quiet world turned into a nightmare.

Vicki had just arrived home from Lone Cedar when she got the call to go back. The co-owner, her manager Ron, and her bartender Riley had walked out only minutes before. Without traffic, which she wouldn't hit in the wee hours of the night, she could drive to the restaurant in about seven-to-eight minutes. *How could something possibly have happened in that short amount of time?*

The restaurant held her family's legacy with a lifetime of memories. The restaurant walls were adorned with memories, photos from her great-granddad's days, while family antiques took a predominant place in the décor. She jumped in her truck, and as she headed across the Nags Head-Manteo Causeway, she noticed the flames.

Witness a Legacy in Flames

In her work clothes, Vicki watched the blaze spread across the building. The fire team consisting of 55 firefighters battled the fire for two hours to get it under control. Basnight's Lone Cedar Restaurant with the family's entire legacy burned to the ground.

"With the knotty pine, it went up fast." Years later, Vicki's voice still quivers as she recalls that heart-wrenching moment. "If we had stayed five minutes longer in the building, we wouldn't have made it out the FBI Agent told me."

Focus on One Blessing

When one of the security sensors triggered, Vicki's mom got the call. Mrs. Basnight saw the flames from her house.

"My father's entire history was in there. Our family-related history that we couldn't get back." Vicki stopped, catching her breath. "Fortunately, when the explosion happened, no one was hurt or injured. Others have gone through worse than we have, because no one was hurt. We focused on that one blessing."

Although suspicions of arson surfaced, a faulty switch manufactured in China that had triggered several other business fires could've been another possible cause.

During this distressing time, the family already faced heartache as Mrs. Basnight battled cancer. Anyone who has fought cancer, or knows someone who did, understands the devastation the disease has on one's body, the side effects of treatment, and the toll it takes on the patient and the family. Adversity kept mounting.

Unlike Chef Wes who you met in Chapter 8, whose hard times happened at the beginning of the low season, the Basnight's devastation occurred after the multi-day Outer Banks Taste of the Beach Festival and the beginning of high season. Vicki had banquets, weddings, and parties scheduled, deposits paid, and revenue projected.

The burned building ignited additional challenges. The fire caused over one million dollars in loss. With the restaurant gone, Lone Cedar's co-owner and her staff of more than 100 people wouldn't receive a paycheck, and the interior insurance payout only covered the cost of two ovens.

How would everyone support themselves? How would the family rebuild?

Discover an Unusual Turning Point

The family's loss didn't end. A month after the fire, Mrs. Basnight sadly lost her battle with cancer. Needing time to mourn, Vicki, along with her sister and their pets, drove to Maine. They spent three weeks grieving before they traveled back to North Carolina.

"We came back for dad," Vicki said. "Dad's drive to rebuild our heritage inspired us. We knew we had to rebuild Lone Cedar for dad if not for anyone else…and for our mom's memory."

A determined Mr. Basnight—a politician at the time— pledged his house as collateral to rebuild the restaurant.

Community Pulls Together

During the fire's clean-up, the Outer Banks (OBX) Community Foundation pitched in, and the OBX community pulled together. Other restaurant owners opened their doors to keep

Lone Cedar's staff working while under construction. "The owners gave Basnight's staff summer jobs, knowing they would come back once Lone Cedar reopened."

This one incredible act revealed the conviction of the community, considering the cost of hiring employees— including her manager and bartender, the two people who were with the restaurant co-owner on that fateful night. The other restaurant owners took on the expense of training additional employees for short-term hire.

During the rebuild, Mr. Basnight traveled to special places he shared with his wife. During these trips, he bought items he knew Mrs. Basnight would like to feature at Lone Cedar and replaced the collectibles his wife had purchased over the years.

OBX Supporters Give

"Almost every piece of décor in Lone Cedar came from members of our community." Vicki's voice trembled as she shared. "They gave family photos celebrating birthdays, holidays like Mother's Day, and weddings. They shared their family history with us. It was so emotional and heartfelt."

When Lone Cedar rebuilt and reopened, their strong customer base supported them. Families came for Sunday dinner. Families booked events again. Community members who didn't have the money to eat out donated family memorabilia for Lone Cedar.

"Our staff and our community members consider us one big extended family," Vicki said, "and we feel that way about them."

Vicki's Bounce-Up Momentum

- Vicki ignored the alarming possibility that arson occurred. Instead, she concentrated on the blessing that no one was hurt.
- Her dad's drive and determination inspired and motivated her. When she realized how much it meant to her dad to rebuild the family legacy, she left Maine and returned home.
- Accept help when given. Vicki gratefully accepted the volunteer workforce offered and the family legacy others shared.

Vicki's Bounce-Up Power

Vicki believed in people and her community. Her firm belief that people are good helped her focus on her blessings. She nurtured relationships within her community, which showed in the way the people assisted in the rebuild, from the fire clean-up to memorabilia.

Vicki's Game Changers: Support Is Your Foundation

1. Look for the silver lining. The only way to get through it, a devastating time—think of the positive. Although we lost our family's heirlooms, **you can't replace a life**. "We [Vicki, Ron, and Riley] walked out alive. That was a silver lining."

2. Concentrate on the support. By ignoring the possibility of someone being so malicious that he would commit arson, Vicki concentrated on the loving support of her community and how the OBX Community pulled together.

3. Believe in fate. Don't ask, "why me?" Ask, "why not me?" Vicki believes there's a reason for everything that happens in life. The fire occurred when her mom was at the end of her life. Rebuilding Lone Cedar and preserving his wife's memory and family legacy gave Mr. Basnight a focus while grieving. In finding pieces of Mrs. Basnight's collection, Mr. Basnight relived happier days he had with his wife.

Bounce-Up Factor:
Create Community Connection

1. What relationships need more nurturing?
2. How can you build stronger relationships within your community?
3. How can you connect to a project that helps someone else?
4. What is one takeaway you gained from this chapter?
5. What is one positive action you will take?

CHAPTER 14
Change Your Life: Find People Who Believe in You

"It doesn't matter how low you fall. It's how high you Bounce-Up" – **Mjism**

Sometimes you need to hear someone's circumstances to understand the growth a person achieved.

Born in 1949, Phil Cohen grew up in a Jewish family in Chicago. The family moved a lot. Most of the neighborhoods were filled with gangs who hated Jewish people. Violence surfaced in every aspect of Phil's life. His father, a troubled man, was in and out of mental hospitals. A womanizer, on drugs and alcohol, Mr. Cohen would make his son strip down in front of the family and beat him. Phil watched his mom attempt suicide four times. Leaving home in his late teens, Phil went searching for something, though he didn't know what. Unfortunately, Phil found himself becoming like his dad.

"I was a womanizer, strung out on drugs, and spent several years homeless," Phil admitted. Fired from seven jobs, Phil was still searching.

"In 1974, I was living in a commune. I had an encounter with God. It turned my life around. The first thing I did when I had found God: I paid people back. I knew I could go to prison for some things I had done. I wanted a clear conscience."

Fortunately, the people involved gave Phil grace when he made amends. Phil changed as his faith deepened. His search continued. "I had a heavy desperation to have a family, a family that loved each other. I didn't have that growing up."

Do What You Need to Do

Phil met his soon-to-be wife in the commune. In 1976, they married and moved into a 24 x 24 rough timber house, without insulation, in a rural area. "We started out pretty raw. We didn't have money for food. We raised and canned everything we ate. I would get wheat and corn from the farmers, hand-grind it to make bread, and bake it in the wood cookstove."

As Phil's personal and financial struggle continued, he found he could make things out of wood, and woodworking became his therapy. He crafted toy trucks, porch swings, birdhouses, and baby cradles. Phil's wife painted the art on the wooden trucks they sold for $10 and made the quilts for the cradles that could bring as much as $100.

"I couldn't believe that I could make things out of wood that would make people happy. I believed I was living a lie and I had them fooled. People could get what I made better and cheaper by someone else, but they kept coming back." Amazement edged into his tone. "I had people who believed in me because I didn't believe in myself. I didn't realize I had something. It wasn't until we started winning national awards that I believed I knew what I was doing."

Clear Out What You Don't Want

As Phil supplemented his woodworking income with odd jobs, the leftover material, and debris accumulated on his property.

"I was doing different things, hard labor for farmers, remodeling, and building barns. Our place was trashed. We had old tractors, junk cars, and board piles. I had a neighbor who was really organized. I told my wife I would give my neighbor $500 to get me organized. I didn't have $500," Phil confessed, "but I knew if he helped me get organized, I'd probably be able to come up with $500."

One day my wife said she could help me get organized and wouldn't charge me anything. "Just figure out what you want to do with your life and get rid of everything else." We started clearing stuff out. If we couldn't sell it, we'd give it away. If we couldn't give it away, we'd throw it away."

Although Phil hadn't figured out what he wanted to do, yet, his business started evolving when he cleared the trash.

Discover the Heart of a Craftsman

Dividing his time and energy between farm labor, building barns, and remodeling, Phil didn't have time to think about what he really wanted to do. He had a family to feed. While working on a kitchen project for a local resident Phil's answer to his wife's question came unexpectedly.

"As I was cutting the parts for the cabinets, I cried. I found what I wanted to do with my life—it was crafting wood cabinets. I cried several times through that job."

Phil found his aha moment and his niche. Now with four children, Phil worked one job to the next. Desperate to make his woodworking business successful, he read everything he could about building cabinets. When he ran out of books, he started calling craftsmen in the industry.

"I called one cabinet maker about 30 miles away. We both had the flu at the time. We'd talk late into the night. He had apprenticed with a German cabinet maker. One night he offered to teach me woodworking. For the next five years, over the phone, he taught me how to make cabinets."

Phil learned about more than cabinetry. "My mentor's shop burned down. He went bankrupt. He didn't think he'd make it. He was building cabinets in his garage. One night he said, 'My skills are in my heart, not my tools.' That was a defining moment for both of us," Phil shared with emotion. "He gave me the heart of a craftsman."

Persistence Pays Off
Working from one project to the next, financial struggles persisted for Phil's family. Phil continued reading books for self-improvement and business success. He listened to audio books, watched videos, and enrolled in self-development programs.

The tipping point for Cohen Architectural Woodworking came from a Boy Scout headquarters project contracted by Bencor Construction Company, formerly owned by senator Bob Corker. The success of the Boy Scout project landed Cohen Woodworking a large Walmart project, as the company was constructing regional stores.

"We got in on the ground floor," says Phil, "and built more than 850 Walmart stores."

Help Others Bounce-Up
Going from a company of one to a company of many requires hiring. Phil wondered who would work for him. Would his background be an issue? I didn't think anyone would want to work for me, so I hired people nobody wanted to hire—people like me who were traumatized."

Phil and his future employees would have a common denominator, a past consisting of drugs, alcohol, or prison. "I believe a company is like a village. In my role as mayor of the village, I have a responsibility to the people." In his duty to his people, Phil asked, *How can we help people have a better family life?* "We want them [employees] to have peace of mind. We want to send them home feeling good."

To set the groundwork for this to happen, Cohen Architectural Woodworking instituted a three-tier program to help their employees develop personally and professionally.

- Tier One: The company carries you. Participants are in a victim state. "Through the classes, they realize life gets better when they get better."
- Tier Two: Cohen Woodworking teaches employees that they must take responsibility. At this level, employees take responsibility for their growth. When employees master this concept, they climb to the next level. "The least likely people have some of the highest positions in the company," Phil shared.
- Tier Three: Employees teach others. They've developed the capacity to help others. When employees reach this level, they are teaching and leading others.

With Phil's mission to help his employees create better family lives, the company contributes $1,000 when employees buy or build their first house. "We offer Dave Ramsey's Financial Peace University, and we teach the Franklin-Covey Life Wheel, which is most effective."

Phil knows he's making a difference when one of his employees says, "I can change my life."

What's next for Phil? He's writing a book, *The Jesus Experiment: Can Jesus Really Run a Business,* to be released in 2020.

Phil's Bounce-Up Momentum

- In the beginning, Phil realized woodworking was therapy. He enjoyed working with his hands.
- Phil's search to give his family a better life propelled him to learn more about the woodworking business, which led him to his mentor.
- Intentionally, Phil hired people like him, which worked best for his company.
- To create positive experiences for his staff, Phil recognized the need for programs, classes, and benefits that would give employees the knowledge and opportunities to create a better life.

Phil's Bounce-Up Power

Phil's desire for a better life led him to personal and business development and growth. He understood when he got better, everyone would get better. He knew how important it was to believe in his employees the way others believed in him.

Phil's Game Changers:
Set Yourself Up for Success

1. Get yourself Mountain Guides. Find people, aka Mountain Guides, who have the scars and experiences to do what you want to do because they've traveled the path. They're not telling you what to do because they read a book. They're telling you what to do because they lived through it. By helping you, they're able to redeem the pain they've experienced.

2. Create a personal growth plan. What character, professional, or business improvements do you need to make? Know what areas you need to develop and grow. Research the actions required to achieve your goal and create a growth plan. Include books, podcasts, and YouTube videos in your plan.

3. Sharpen your saw. Phil learned the value of making your morning count when he lived in the country. If he didn't take the time to sharpen the saw before he started the lumber job, it could take 10 hours. By spending the hour to sharpen the saw just right, the job would take only three hours. What you do in the a.m. determines your day. Make your morning count. Put together a plan for the day before your day begins.

Boost Your Bounce-Up Factor:
Start Fresh

1. How would implementing a pre-day planning session make a difference in your day, week, and professional life?

2. What do you need to sell, give away, or throw away to be more focused?

3. What personal or professional area do you need to develop to grow, and what research do you need to do?
4. What is one takeaway you gained from this chapter?
5. What is one positive action you will take?

Part IV

Together We Can Bounce-Up™

That's a Wrap: Or Is It?

"Your mindset influences your opportunities and outcomes." - **Mjism**

As I was writing my last few chapters of this book, I had my regular six-month mammogram. Expecting to hear "Everything's okay," (after all I was only 18 months out from final treatment) imagine my shock when I had to have a second set of scans and a closed-door talk with the radiologist. Three weeks later, a biopsy confirmed the calcifications were recurrent invasive cancer—minuscule, though invasive cancer, which would warrant more surgeries.

I felt like a time warp sucked me in. I had the second round of chemotherapy, called Herceptin, which was supposed to decrease the recurrence to seven percent over seven years. I had seven weeks of daily radiation to kill any rogue cells after the first surgery. Well, that obviously didn't work. Plus, I was taking the recommended daily chemo pill. Add to this, after receiving the first diagnosis, I followed the three recommendations: 7–8 hours of sleep, 3–5 fruits and veggies daily, and regular exercise to avoid recurrence.

All I could do was shake my head. Well, I cried, too. The memory of the 13-month treatment plan with all the nasty side effects hadn't completely faded. Plus, I'm writing a book about Bouncing-Up, and I'm dumbfounded that I received a second cancer diagnosis so soon. My kids couldn't believe it. They shared they were mad that it happened again. Verbal Drama attacked. I knew better, and yet, that nasty Inner Drama happened. It was too new.

Rely on Your Foundation

Though I had continued with business meetings, client training sessions, and mastermind meetings, it took about two weeks before I flipped my Verbal Drama during a conversation with Andrea Hart, a long-time friend and one of my Power Team members. (I do practice what I recommend.)

"Imagine how big it would be if you hadn't done all those things to keep it away? The calcifications were the size of a grain of rice because you did all those things," said Andrea.

Our conversation was a blessing. I had faith, a supportive family, and a strong Power Team, including an experienced medical team of doctors, RNs, patient care technicians (PCTs), and so many more, whom I trusted.

I carried my gratefulness and positive outlook into surgery and the short hospital stay. I also had several business magazines to keep my mind occupied. While there, I watched how the medical staff ran their butts off, taking care of me and everyone else. I saw the extra work they endured when someone had to be taken to the Intensive Care Unit (ICU), or someone decided to be a mean old grouch. I could hear the nastiness coming from some of the rooms as I walked the hall. Psst…Please remember to thank any medical staff providing healthcare for you or your family.

During the hospital stay, I thanked the staff and asked questions about them. One of the residents had a baby girl five weeks prior, moved to Pittsburgh from Nashville for her residency, and her husband was a first-year resident, too. Wow, that's crazy! We never know someone else's journey until we ask. I learned one nurse was 69 and thinking about retiring, and her daughter had the same surgery. One RN had a family dairy farm. As I talked to one of the PCTs about favorite colors because I wore a purple robe, she shared she recently had purple hair that got washed out when she went swimming.

My curiosity about people created fascinating conversations. Also, I wanted to talk about something other than vitals, IVs, and all the other nuances involved. Without intending to do so, I made it about them and not about me. I hadn't realized how this small shift changed their days until one of the surgeons scheduled my discharge. (I got discharged two days early because I was doing too well to keep me. Imagine my big grin.)

Jackie, the nighttime 69-year-old soon-to-retire RN, said, "You, patients like you, remind me why I'm still a nurse."

As Meghan, the daytime RN, gave me the discharge papers, she said, "I will always remember you."

"Why?" I asked, thinking she sees thousands of people a year.

"Your attitude was such a joy to be around."

Those questions, which turned into Momentum Questions, shifted attitudes for all of us.

Be Ready for Adversity
President Jim Tressel said, "it isn't **if** adversity hits, it's **when**." Well, it hit again. Now, I needed to work with what I had. Before the surgery, I outlined a plan of what I could do to maintain my business while being restricted from working and driving for six weeks. **Six. Weeks.** I'll admit, at first, I balked when I heard I could NOT do either for six weeks. I cried off and on for the first two days. I gave in to the emotions and allowed myself to feel them. You can't go through a life-altering event, **let alone three in less than one**

decade, without having some emotions surfacing. The issue becomes when we remain in that emotional vortex. When we linger in the negative vacuum, we keep the clouds overhead.

After my initial shock, definitely a shock, I developed a business maintenance plan. When you're the business, if you don't work, there isn't revenue coming in. Thank goodness for services like Uber, Lyft, ZOOM, InstaCart, and Amazon Prime. Yes, I used all of them. (I had a personal plan, too, with the love, support and help of my three kids, Deanna, Josh, and Kristy. Yes, I consider my daughter-in-law Kristy one of my kids.)

Brainstorm a Game Plan

Throughout *Bounce-Up*, I talk about being unshakable, building momentum, and creating a plan. Well, here was another opportunity to put my words into practice. (Please note, I did follow most of the recommendations. The last thing I wanted was to spiral downward because I pushed too hard.)

Below you'll see the outcome of that business maintenance plan.

- I borrowed four business books I wanted to read from the library. Besides watching animated movies with the g-kiddies and binge-watching superhero movies, reading was one of the only activities I could manage in the first week.
- With the United States map in hand, I charted which states and organizations would work best for a book tour. This task was a fun activity. With pink, orange, and green highlighters, I marked the cities on the map.

- Using Lyft and Uber starting in week two, I meet with a colleague for coffee once a week and increased it as I felt stronger. This action enabled me to keep my business brain active, enjoy the company of others, and keep restlessness at bay.
- I completed the front matter, back resources, and a few interviews for this book, *Bounce-Up*.
- With the notes I jotted, I outlined the *Bounce-Up* workbook, which will be great for workshops.
- Finalizing my marketing materials for my *Bounce-Up* keynote, I sent the project to my graphic designer.
- While surfing social media, I pulled conferences where I could present a workshop or give my keynote and put them into a computer file for later.
- I edited website pages for a client and outlined a training segment for another client.

By focusing on the designated tasks, it kept my mind off the unpleasant aftermath of the surgery. Remember the tactic I mentioned earlier, *get busy, get better*.

Although my original action plan was much bigger than the outcomes listed above, when I wrote this list of accomplishments, I was thrilled. (If you're like me, you probably have a list longer than what is genuinely possible.) We don't always spend time reviewing our accomplishments. Remember the Super-Size-You Powers activity. Even tackling one feat would be an advantage.

Also, for me, this was the creative part of what I do, and I don't spend as much time as I'd like to devote to the creative side when I am training organizations or speaking at conferences. Plus, I love my work, so it never seems like work to me. Being strategic and pre-planning, I feel made the difference because I focused on projects and solutions.

Life's knockdowns will always happen. It isn't about the knockdown; it's about how we Bounce-Up™. You CAN do it!

Here's to a future of outpowering adversity, boosting resilience, and bouncing-up.

Mj Callaway

P.S. Please share your Bounce-Up™ stories with me at www.FaceBook.com/Bounce-UpCommunity

Momentum Builders/Discussion Questions

For business teams and board retreats, pre-select questions to discuss. Then, break into smaller groups of two or three. Give each pair/trio specific questions to answer. Set a designated amount of time. When the time is up, have one person from each team be the spokesperson. In a round-robin format, the spokesperson will share what his or her team discovered.

For small groups and book clubs, create an interactive discussion by having one person lead. This person will prompt the questions and responses.

1. How else could you use the tools, tactics, and techniques in this book to help you Bounce-Up? What specific tactics could your team use to hit your targeted goals?
2. Which section or chapter of Bounce-Up resonated the most with you? Is there anyone else that found the same section/chapter as valuable as you did?
3. What success story resonated the most with you? Who else resonates with the same success story as you did? Did it resonate with each of you for the same reason? Discuss the reason it resonates with each of you.
4. Which of the roadblocks did you recognize in yourself and/or your team? How has this roadblock stopped you/your team from reaching targeted goals in the past?
5. What is one action you/your team can take to eliminate roadblocks?
6. Have you ever let Verbal Drama keep you spinning in the same place? Have you ever let Verbal Drama about your team or organization cause you to be stuck?

7. In Chapter 7, there are two examples of people with conviction. Who is someone you know who has faced the odds and Bounced-Up? How can you use this example as a positive way to move you or your organization forward?

8. What is a common personal or professional situation that creates chaos for you?

9. How can a Power Team influence positive actions in your organization? Within 30 days, can you create your Power Team? Who would be on your Power Team?

10. How can you incorporate more positive energy into your day or your organization's environment?

11. What training, coaching, or mentoring can help you Bounce-Up?

12. What will you do differently today to build momentum?

Bounce-Up™ Wordology, aka Glossary

Aimable: A specific deadline you can target to reach your goal.

BHAG: Big Hairy Audacious Goal that can be out of reach.

Boyfriend: Mj used boyfriend as a term to replace the word IV.

Bounce-Up™: Instead of bouncing back, you Bounce-Up higher and stronger than before.

Buzz: Mj replaced the word radiation with the word Buzz. When she thought of the word Buzz, she would think of Buzz Lightyear and it made her smile.

Conviction: You have extreme confidence and belief in your ability to achieve something meaningful.

Disruption: An event that interrupts your life because it causes change, chaos, and loss.

Emotional Meaning: Emotional Meaning provides a heartfelt reason to achieve a goal.

Fear: Fear grips you like one of those sticky monster balls kids throw against the wall, and it sticks.

Hacky Sack: An analogy used for the Immobility roadblock.

Power Team: Trusted people in your life you can count on to be your champion, cheerleader, and supporter.

Ignitor: A person who ignites action.

Immobility: Stuck in the same spot, as a hacky sack without action.

Improvise: Create alternative ways to get a task or project completed.

Magic Wand: Mj viewed chemotherapy as the magic wand being waved to get rid of the Pink Pumpkin.

Mental Drive: The tunnel-vision focus that enables you to reach your goal.

Pink Pumpkin: Mj replaced the word cancer/tumor with Pink Pumpkin.

Self-Efficacy: Believe in your abilities to succeed.

Sticky Monster Ball: An analogy used for the Fear roadblock.

Sticky Monster Ball, Hacky Sack, and Superball Syndrome: A fun analogy used when referring to the three roadblocks: Fear, Immobility, and Verbal Drama.

Stretch Goal: A challenging goal you can strive to hit.

Superball: An analogy used for the Verbal Drama roadblock.

Super-Size-You: An activity that enables you to uncover your core strengths, talents, and traits.

Unshakability: Your belief that your strengths, ability, and determination will help you overcome adversity.

Verbal Drama: The self-talk consisting of all the inner dialogue and drama why you can't reach a goal or your potential.

National Resources

Alex's Lemonade Stand Foundation
www.AlexsLemonade.org

American Cancer Society
www.cancer.org
800-227-2345

American Counseling Association
www.counseling.org

American Heart Association
www.heart.org
800-242-8721

National Speakers Association
www.NSASpeaker.org

Substance Abuse and Mental Health Services Administration
https://www.samhsa.gov/find-help/national-helpline
800-662-HELP

U.S. Department of Health and Human Services: Mental Health
www.mentalhealth.gov

Women's Business Enterprise National Council
www.wbenc.org

Acknowledgements

There are numerous people behind the author of every book. As I acknowledge the people who supported, guided, and encouraged me throughout this project, my business, and challenges over the past three years, there are many more people that have been a part of my Power Team over the past decade—more people than I could acknowledge.

To my editor Margaret Hewitt and illustrator Shannon Zadrozny: a big thank you for your expertise. We did it!

A huge thank you to Vicki Basnight, Phil Cohen, Pam Kinzler, Summer Owens, Sarah Souri, Wes Stepp, and Jim Tressel for seeing my vision as I created this book and allowing me to share your stories. When it comes to Bouncing-Up, you rock!

To Quinn Capps for the interview introductions that added depth to my book. The way you uplift others warms my heart.

Thank you to Julie Ann Sullivan for introducing me to Phil Cohen, your NSA wisdom and coffee meetings.

To Elizabet Rodriguez: you will always be in my heart.

To my clients who give me the opportunity to share my messages from sales to resilience with you. Let's rock the revenue streams.

To my Confluence Mastermind and business family: Joe Mull, Kathy Parry, Renee Thompson, and Jeff Tobe for providing your support, resources, mentoring, and answers to grow all aspects of my business. A heartfelt thank you for all you have done and your Influence 2017 gift.

Acknowledgements

To my Tri-State Power Women's Mastermind: Debbie Peterson, Lisa Ryan, and Maureen Zappala for helping me dig deeper into my programs, your kick-a$$-get-it-done strategies, and cheering me on. A big hug to each of you.

To my Medical Power Team: Dr. Carolyn de La Cruz, Dr. Emilia Diego, Dr. Marsha Haley, Dr. Seungwon Kim, Dr. Dhaval R. Metha, PA-C Kelly Nicholas, PA-C Jessie A. Starr and your amazing teams; thank you for your expertise and answering hundreds of questions. ☺

To RNs and PCTs on the 5800 Floor at Magee Women's Hospital: you do so much for so many. Thank you for your dedication.

To my wonderful "Chin Up, Be There" Power Team: Bob Pacanovsky, Kimber Braswell, Andrea Hart, Bonnie Artman Fox, Laura Crooks, Georgianna Koulianos, Eric Kulikowski, Kelly Salonica Staikopoulos, Toni Saul, Tawnya Senchur, and Christina Sylvester.

To the fabulous Beverly Breton Carroll: a huge thank you for always being on my Power Team, thank you for your friendship, wisdom, laughter, and hours of discussion as we traveled this professional and personal self-development journey during the past twenty-some years.

To the best kids a mom could have and the first in my Power Team: Deanna, Josh, and Kristy; for your love, TLC, and always believing in me. I am because of you. You make my heart swell with love, joy, and pride.

To my g-kiddies: Ziggy, Ayla, Jeremiah, and Sophia. You bring endless laughter, joy and love to my life. Praise God for these cherished moments.

Above all, faith has been my foundation and strength to Bounce-Up™.

Reference Notes

Chapter 1

- Clarkson, Kelly. "Stronger (What Doesn't Kill You)." https://www.youtube.com/watch?v=avYxiIRG4xQ.
- National Opinion Research Center at University of Chicago. "Survey Shows Americans' Personal Misery Has Increased Since Early 1990s." University of Chicago News Office. December 28, 2005. http://www-news.uchicago.edu/releases/05/051228.troubles.shtml.
- "Rocky Balboa Motivational Speech to His Son." https://www.goalcast.com/2016/04/15/rocky-balboa-motivational-speech-son.

Chapter 2

- Azpiri, Jon, and Paul Johnson. "Apple Co-Founder Sold His Shares for $800. Today They'd Be Worth $94 billion. He Regrets Nothing." *Global News.* April 14, 2019. https://globalnews.ca/news/5158415/apple-co-founder-ronald-wayne.
- Hay, Louise. "Meditation." https://www.louisehay.com/tag/meditation.

Chapter 3

- Ballparks of Baseball. "Minute Maid Park." www.BallparksofBaseball.com.
- IMDb. "Christina Ricci." https://www.imdb.com/name/nm0000207.
- Lavine, Lindsay. "Is Your Brain Hardwired to Be Negative? Why That Might Be A Good Thing." *Fast Company.* May 6, 2014. https://www.fastcompany.com/3030026/is-your-brain-hardwired-to-be-negative-why-that-might-be-a-good-thing.
- Mays, Robert. "Jalen Ramsey Is the NFL's Most Relentless Trash Talker." *The Ringer.* November 16, 2017. https://www.theringer.com/nfl/2017/11/16/16658816/jalen-ramsey-jacksonville-jaguars-trash-talk.
- Osteen, Joel. *I Declare: 31 Promises to Speak Over Your Life.* Nashville: FaithWords, 2012.

Reference Notes

Chapter 4

- Brooks, Alison Wood. "Get Excited: Reappraising Pre-Performance Anxiety as Excitement." *Journal of Experimental Psychology* 143, no. 3 (2014): 1144-1158. https://www.apa.org/pubs/journals/releases/xge-a0035325.pdf.
- Cuddy, Amy. "Your iPhone is Ruining Your Posture — And Your Mood." *New York Times.* December 12, 2015.
- Marchand, Andrew. "Inside Dirt: Aaron Judge Has a Secret Plan to Break His Slump." *ESPN.* July 18, 2017. https://www.espn.com/mlb/story/_/id/20091290/here-dirt-new-york-yankees-aaron-judge.
- Wallace, Christina. "The Three Questions That Can Help You Get Outside Your Head and Identify Your Superpower." *Forbes.* September 17, 2017. https://www.forbes.com/sites/christinawallace/2017/09/17/the-three-questions-that-can-help-you-get-outside-your-head-and-identify-your-superpower/#650192db6e5d.
- Wendell, Emely. "iHunch." American Bone Health. February 3, 2017. https://americanbonehealth.org/nutrition/ihunch.

Chapter 5

- Katz, Andy. "Spurs Feel Fortunate to Draft Blair in Second." *ESPN.* June 26, 2009. http://www.espn.com/mens-college-basketball/blog/_/name/katz_andy/id/4288788/nba-draft-surprise-pittsburgh-panthers-duo-falling-second-round.
- Readability Formulas. www.ReadabilityFormulas.com.

Chapter 6

- Anwar, Yasmin. "Figuring Out How Gizmos Work." *Berkeley News.* March 6, 2014. https://news.berkeley.edu/2014/03/06/figuring-out-how-gizmos/https://news.berkeley.edu/2014/03/06/ figuring-out-how-gizmos.
- Cranford, James. "DSM-IV Alcohol Dependence and Marital Dissolution: Evidence from the National Epidemiologic Survey on Alcohol and Related Conditions." *Journal of Studies on Alcohol and Drugs* 11, no. 3 (May 2014): 520-529. http://www.jsad.com/toc/jsad/75/3.

- Dintino, Cecilia. "Can Improvisation Change Your Life?" *Psychology Today*. March 8, 2018. https://www.psychologytoday.com/us/blog/midlife-matters/201803/can-improvisation-change-your-life.
- Seelig, Tina. "How to Catch Luck." TED Talk filmed at TED NYC June 2018. www.tinaseelig.com.
- SelfBrand. www.selfbrand.com.
- Shontell, Alyson. "After 10 Months, A Boatload of Press, and a CEO's Departure, Apparel Startup Quincy Shuts Down." *Business Insider*. January 28, 2013. https://www.businessinsider.com/after-10-months-a-boatload-of-press-and-a-ceos-departure-apparel-startup-quincy-shuts-down-2013-1.
- Wallace, Christina. "The Three Questions That Can Help You Get Outside Your Head and Identify Your Superpower." *Forbes*. September 17, 2017. https://www.forbes.com/sites/christinawallace/2017/09/17/the-three-questions-that-can-help-you-get-outside-your-head-and-identify-your-superpower/#650192db6e5d.

Chapter 7
- Biography. "Bethany Hamilton Biography." Updated April 12, 2019. https://www.biography.com/athlete/bethany-hamilton.
- Hamilton, Bethany. "Biography." https://bethanyhamilton.com/biography.
- Rodriguez, Nancy. "Bethany Hamilton is Unstoppable." *Santa Barbara Independent*. March 22, 2019. https://www.independent.com/2019/03/22/bethany-hamilton-is-unstoppable.
- Yam, Kimberly. "Girl Who Wore Hot Dog Costume to Princess Week Is Our New Role Model." *Huffpost*. June 6, 2016. https://www.huffpost.com/entry/girl-who-wore-hot-dog-costume-to-princess-week-is-the-cutest-trailblazer_n_575585c8e4b0c3752dce1b4c.

Chapter 9

- Mayo Clinic. "Dystonia." Last modified August 10, 2018. https://www.mayoclinic.org/diseases-conditions/dystonia/symptoms-causes/syc-20350480.

Chapter 10

- Breier, Eric. "From Teen Mom to College Graduate." California State University San Marcos New Center. May 8, 2017. https://news.csusm.edu/from-teen-mom-to-college-graduate.
- Hechinger Report. "Fewer Teen Moms but Still a Dropout Puzzle for Schools." January 22, 2018. https://www.usnews.com/news/national-news/articles/2018-01-22/fewer-teenage-mothers-but-they-still-present-a-dropout-puzzle-for-schools.

Chapter 14

- Ramsey, Dave. "Financial Peace University." www.DaveRamsey.com.

About Mj Callaway

Mj Callaway is a pro at motivating people and organizations. As an award-winning author, motivational speaker, and corporate trainer, Mj has two sweet spots: resilience and sales. One must be resilient to be a two-time survivor and have the sales savvy to be the top-producing sales executive in a male-dominated industry. Mix in that Mj started over with only $500 when her safety became jeopardized.

To help others succeed, she shares inspirational stories from people from all walks of life to offer strategic tools to outpower adversity, crush change, and elevate success. She knows firsthand the disruptions teams, managers, and executives handle daily. Yet, they still need to perform, produce, and hit those projections. She understands the power of "a single word" and shows audience members how they can develop powerful verbal and non-verbal tools to use.

Mj blends two worlds, sales and journalism, to create interactive and impactful workshops. With eight books written, including two Warner Books best-sellers, and over 2,000 articles published in consumer magazines, she's interviewed hundreds of people from youth entrepreneurs to CEOs to nonprofit founders to professional athletes. She has a unique ability to make audiences feel like they're talking to a friend.

She's earned four Gold Awards from Parenting Media Association (PMA), One Bronze Award from PMA, and Member of the Year from National Speakers Association Pittsburgh. Mj travels the country, presenting keynotes and workshops to show organizations how they can create a contagious upbeat attitude with her "What's next" game plan.

A few fun facts about Mj: She's zip-lined over gators in Gulf Shores, Alabama, played tug-a-war over a backpack with a baby black bear in the UP of Michigan, and biked down a volcano in Maui.

Connect with Mj:
www.MjCallaway.com
Mj@MjCallaway.com
LinkedIn: MjCallaway
Twitter: @MjCallawaySpeak
Facebook: MjCallawaySpeaker

Ready for a dynamic speaker with immediate "implementable" strategies for your next conference, retreat, or training?

- Is your organization facing disruptions from infrastructure changes, economic downturn, or personal challenges?

- Are sales or productivity quotas stalled, or worse yet, tumbling?

- Do you want your audience to build momentum toward goals and increase productivity?

If you answered "yes" to any of these questions, **email Mj at Mj@MjCallaway.com**.

Mj's customized programs aren't cookie cutter or prepackaged. Participants get proven tactics and techniques they can apply immediately. That's the reason corporations book Mj two, three and four times for keynotes, training, and workshops. With humorous anecdotes, interactive activities and real-world experiences, Mj engages your audience and equips them to Bounce-Up their resilience, results, and revenue.

Isn't it time for your organization to Bounce-Up?!

To book Mj or learn more about her programs, **visit MjCallaway.com**.

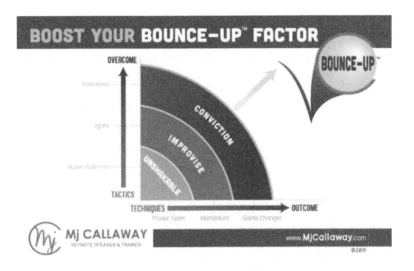

When your team needs a Conceptual Model for positive and productive change, contact Mj Callaway

Index

162

Index

Made in the USA
Las Vegas, NV
23 March 2022